Praise for *Bridging the Gap*

"*Bridging the Gap* provides readers with invaluable resources on how to support a neurodivergent workforce. Judson's use of strengths-based language when describing neurodivergent professionals emphasizes how important it is for managers to support neurodivergent colleagues across the hiring cycle, from the initial job description to onboarding and beyond. While this book is particularly helpful for hiring managers, college and university career centers, and neurodivergent individuals, it will also be incredibly helpful for anyone wishing to broaden their knowledge of supporting and retaining diverse candidates across all industry sectors."

—**LAUREN A. BURROWS, M.Ed.**, director, Saint Anselm College Career Development Center

"As the father of a twenty-four-year-old son with autism and cochair of Friends of South Florida Autism, I've spent over twenty years navigating the complex and often misunderstood world of neurodiversity. *Bridging the Gap* is an invaluable resource filled with actionable insights to help both employers and neurodivergent employees succeed in the workplace. This book offers a clear, thoughtful roadmap for organizations seeking to build more inclusive, productive environments and fully tap into the unique strengths of this talented population. Having spent thirty-plus years in the corporate world, I know that onboarding is still an inconsistent practice with too much variability, so the recommendations in this book will benefit neurotypical individuals, too. I wholeheartedly recommend this guide to employers, parents, educators, and anyone committed to fostering meaningful inclusion."

—**JOSE "JOE" L. MIR,** cochair, Friends of South Florida Autism, and CEO, Mir Strategic Solutions

"*Bridging the Gap* is an excellent and concise guide to the world of work for neurodivergent employees and job seekers, managers who supervise neurodivergent team members, and organizations that employ neurodivergent staff. Judson provides practical advice concerning the recruitment, onboarding, and supervision of neurodivergent individuals. The recommendations and strategies she provides are not only applicable to neurodivergent employees and their employers; any organization would benefit from implementing these practices across the board. Employers should work toward creating a neuro-inclusive environment both for the benefit of their employees and the many other rewards— such as increased productivity—that neuro-inclusivity brings to a business. This book is a useful guide to achieving a neuro-inclusive organization."

—**LAWRENCE E. SAUER,** chief executive officer, League School for Autism

"As a coach for neurodiverse adults, I recommend *Bridging the Gap* for its invaluable and actionable insights. This book goes beyond theory, offering a practical, empathetic roadmap for both managers and employees navigating the complexities and strengths of neurodiversity in professional environments. Judson draws from her dual perspective as a successful corporate leader and a parent of neurodiverse children who have thrived in the workforce. Her unique lens brings authenticity and relevance to the strategies she presents. This guide resonates deeply with the experiences of the individuals I support, and I've seen firsthand how its tools and approaches can empower neurodivergent professionals to succeed."

—**JEAN SANDLER,** MSW, senior clinical director, Association for Autism and Neurodiversity

"Lee Judson has a remarkable ability to meet individuals where they are, especially those who feel overlooked and those who are seeking guidance as they navigate the nuances of the workplace. In *Bridging the Gap*, Judson brings that same clarity, compassion, and strategic insight to the page. Blending lived experience with practical tools, she offers a timely and empowering guide for organizations ready to move from awareness to true inclusion. This is the playbook every forward-thinking leader needs."

—**ALISHA MAGNUS-LOUIS,** chief strategy officer, *The Los Angeles Tribune*

"*Bridging the Gap* is a great way to start conversations with any company developing a program focused on the hiring, onboarding, and ongoing support of neurodiverse employees. It is also a valuable guidebook for neurodivergent individuals and their families, with solid tips for success in their first jobs and beyond. I'll be sharing this much-needed resource with my network."

—**KRISTINE BIAGIOTTI,** colead, Dell True Ability Employee Resource Group North America, and vice chair, board of directors, Center of Hope Foundation

"This book offers clear, actionable insights that empower neurodivergent professionals and the people who work with them. It's an essential guide for anyone serious about building neurodivergent-friendly teams that thrive, and it delivers the tools neurodivergent professionals and their managers have been waiting for. Insightful, grounded, and deeply needed—this is the handbook I wish every self-advocate and manager had. A must-read for every workplace."

—**SHEA BELSKY,** autistic self-advocate and people manager

BRIDGING
THE
GAP

BRIDGING
THE
GAP

A FIELD GUIDE TO NEURODIVERSITY AT WORK

for ☑MANAGERS, ☑COLLEAGUES *and*
☑EVERYONE WONDERING
"Is It Just Me?"

LEE JUDSON

Kalman
PRESS

Bridging the Gap: A Field Guide to Neurodiversity at Work for
Managers, Colleagues, and Everyone Wondering "Is It Just Me?"

Copyright 2025, Elisa Judson

ISBN (paperback): 979-8-9998113-0-1
ISBN (e-book): 979-8-9998113-1-8
ISBN (audiobook): 979-8-9998113-2-5

Library of Congress Control Number: 2025920867

Edited by: Scott and Jocelyn Carbonara, Spiritus Books
Cover and interior design by: George Stevens, G Sharp Design

Published by Kalman Press, Sharon, Massachusetts

To my children, who prompted me to dig deeper to discover the wonders and challenges of neurodiversity.

And to anyone who has ever felt misunderstood or locked into their own world because of their neurodivergent mind.

Contents

Foreword

Is it just me?

If you've ever asked yourself that question at work—maybe during a meeting where everyone seemed to be speaking a language you almost understood, or after receiving feedback that didn't reflect your actual contributions—you're not alone. For many neurodivergent professionals, those moments of disconnection are far too common. And even for neurotypical teammates, bridging cognitive style differences can feel like stumbling across an invisible divide.

That's why this book is so timely and so necessary.

Lee Judson has given us more than a field guide. She's given us a new lens. *Bridging the Gap* is smart, practical, and above all, human. It illuminates the hidden friction points that derail performance, undermine trust, and marginalize people, often unintentionally. And it invites us to do better.

I first connected with Lee through her husband, who is a fraternity brother. Decades later, Lee reached out to share her vision for helping students and early-career employees thrive. I was immediately intrigued. That conversation sparked an ongoing collaboration that reflects the power of lifelong networks, shared values, and mutual curiosity.

As someone who helps organizations operationalize performance management, I think about three critical domains. The first is how we *align* people with what success looks like. The second is how we *perform* through consistent coaching and feedback. And the third is how we *boost* results by surfacing insights that help everyone grow. Across all three, clarity is everything.

But clarity isn't uniformity.

Clarity means defining expectations in ways people can actually understand and act on. It means creating room for different kinds of brilliance to show up and thrive. It means replacing generic feedback with specific, forward-focused conversations. It means noticing not just what someone is doing, but how they are wired to get there.

That's the heart of this book. Lee meets the reader with generosity, not judgment. She brings research, personal experience, and practical advice together in a voice that is warm and direct. Whether you're a manager, a teammate, or someone trying to make sense of your own work world, you'll find wisdom here. And, more importantly, you'll discover tools.

Read it. Share it. Reflect on it. Then use it to change something in your workplace. When we design for neurodiversity, we don't just include more people. We build systems that work better for everyone

Joe Rotella

Chief Value Officer, Delphia Consulting
Co-creator of miviva, a system to operationalize performance management
SHRM-SCP, SPHR, CPBA

Introduction

Driving down the freeway on her way to work one fall day, a young woman—let's call her Joan—had an epiphany, just as the song "Hotel California" by the Eagles came on the radio. Turning down the music, she pushed a button to dial the office manager of her department.

"Listen, Betsy," she spoke excitedly into the Bluetooth. "I figured it out. I think I actually dreamed about it last night. But anyway, we just need to *flip the data sets on their sides*. This should give us the information to prove that we do *not* owe the hospital for the claims they say we owe."

Click. The voicemail was left. The world had been saved.

Or so Joan thought.

Arriving that day to the insurance company where she worked, she expected to see Betsy jump in glee that Joan had finally solved the massive problem plaguing their department. Instead, Betsy seemed apathetic—

frustrated even—anything but elated. *Great, here we go again*, Joan thought, deciding her brilliant plans were being completely misconstrued and misunderstood for the umpteenth time.

"Did you even listen to my voicemail?" Joan asked, tired of feeling like the odd one out in her department even though she was the manager.

"I did, but it made no sense! 'Flip the data sets on their sides.' What are you even talking about? It doesn't work like that." Betsy gave Joan a look as if to say, *You utter lunatic.*

Why don't people ever understand me when I speak? Joan thought, handing Betsy the coffee she'd bought her to offset this tough day. "Here, let me show you."

Joan stepped up to Betsy's computer and grabbed the mouse—while failing to notice Betsy's bristling at the intrusion to her personal space. After a few clicks of the keyboard, voilà, sure enough, her epiphany had paid off. There, in plain terms, were the results the department needed to move forward confidently, knowing they did *not* owe money to the hospital.

"See?" Joan asked. "If we use the common key, we can match the claims with the dollars spent for each patient. Put it all into a pivot table to combine the data, and we can show the hospital that we've already paid them for those claims. This table has the amount we charged, this has the amount we paid, and they both have this key that will match them." In effect, sure enough, the data had been *flipped on its side.*

"You're brilliant," Betsy said, half under her breath. "And I hate you. Thank you for the coffee." She finally broke a smile and winked at Joan.

"I know you love me," Joan answered with a smirk. "And you're welcome."

While the two shared a tension-shattering ribbing and joke, Joan reflected on how she didn't always feel valued—or even liked—at work. In fact, she often thought others saw her as the weird fish, swimming in the wrong direction. Laughed at within her "pod," she often felt alone amongst the vicious or gloomy sharks. Her mind worked differently. Sometimes she could solve problems no one else could decipher, but other times she felt like the only one excluded from a big inside joke—like an invisible line had been drawn between her and the rest of the workplace, and she was inadvertently and perpetually placed outside of it. Would she get lost at sea, or could she one day find her "school of fish" and thrive? Which leads to our second example.

That Saturday, Joan had to run errands with her preschool-aged son, Sam. Strapping him into his car seat behind her and leaving their neighborhood, she had an idea.

"Hey buddy, how about on the way home we head to the aquarium?"

Sam didn't give much of a response, but that wasn't atypical for him. He was likely riveted with watching the buildings stream by outside the car window—or counting telephone poles on the way to the freeway—but that didn't mean he hadn't heard her.

Hours of errands passed, and it was time to head home. Joan glanced in the back seat and saw that Sam had fallen asleep. *Shucks*, she thought as she passed the aquarium. *I can't wake him now.* Joan adhered to the cardinal rule of "do not wake your sleeping child."

But having an observant son meant nothing would go unnoticed. Sam woke up, two exits past the aquarium, frustrated and grumpy. He began mumbling something incomprehensible. Limbs probably began flailing.

"What are you trying to tell me?!" Joan asked, mirroring Sam's frustration and completely forgetting about the earlier promise she'd made to him. She heard him say something about *fish* and thought maybe he was hungry for fish and chips. Afterall, they were late for lunch.

"The *building with the FISHES!*" he finally stated angrily, unable to articulate the word *aquarium*, even though he had heard it stated clearly hundreds of times before—and once earlier that day. His tone seemed to imply, *You ignorant witch, how could you not understand the words coming out of my face? How could you forget your promise, the linchpin to this whole day, and the reason I put up with all this boring errand crap in the first place?*

Sam had challenges in preschool and had been diagnosed with dyspraxia. This disorder affects movement, coordination, and speech, and it can also contribute to difficulty learning. Joan and his teachers knew he was as smart as (or smarter than) his friends, but he couldn't articulate his words clearly enough for others to understand. This led to anger outbursts when he was misunderstood. Sam had begun talking "late," and he still wasn't communicating effectively.

Once Sam reached elementary school, Joan and her husband pushed to get him tested more extensively because even though he wasn't like other kids, he clearly possessed brilliance when given the right direction and tasks. He excelled in math and had a high vocabulary, even if he couldn't articulate his thoughts well or put words together to read. Without tapping into the right educational tools, Joan feared he was at risk of drifting like another fish lost at sea. And she especially longed for him to be understood by his teachers.

While the testing showed that Sam struggled with some skills, he scored incredibly high in the IQ exams. After seeing another specialist, he was diagnosed with autism spectrum disorder (ASD), which changed the course of his life. With something more tangible—a lens through which to see his learning abilities, strengths, and challenges—perhaps he could finally find his pod, Joan thought. Even if he was a different "color" or attracted to a different "lure," she hoped he could still contribute to a vibrant ecosystem, wherever that might be.

As Sam was being assessed, Joan and her husband were asked multiple questions.

"Is he a messy eater?"

"No, but our daughter is," Joan answered.

"Is your son able to stay focused on a task when you ask him to?"

"Yes, as a matter of fact, he stays very focused but our daughter does not," Joan's husband responded.

"Is your son a picky, limited eater?" the psychologist asked.

"Umm, no. Our son is willing to try everything, including stealing the sushi from my plate. But ... my daughter only eats chicken nuggets," Joan responded. She and her husband looked at each other, realizing instantly that they needed to have their daughter evaluated as well.

It turned out that their daughter, too, was "different," and soon thereafter got a diagnosis of attention-deficit hyperactivity disorder (ADHD).

After her children's assessments, Joan had her own aha moment. By recognizing their neurodivergence, she was able to see that her own mind wasn't typical either. *That sounds an awful lot like me*, she thought as she read over her daughter's diagnosis. Her daughter was struggling to read, could not keep her room clean, and was always interrupting conversations. Joan suddenly remembered her own childhood—arguing with her mom at the library when she didn't want to take out yet another book, and regularly getting reprimanded for having a messy room.

And Sam's diagnosis sounds a lot like his dad, Joan reflected, putting the pieces together to see the neurodiversity within her family.

As the author of this book, I know Joan and Sam well. That's because I am "Joan," and "Sam" is my son. (No, those aren't our real names, if you haven't guessed by now.) When my son and daughter were diagnosed, it got me thinking about my own potential neurodivergence. When my daughter took her assessment, I actually filled out some of the forms for myself. After some discussions, the PhD psychologist who performed my daughter's exam exclaimed, "She must have gotten her ADHD from you!" And over the years, a few therapists reinforced this thinking for me.

Based on this awareness that my own brain seemed "different," I adjusted how I approached my work and the people around me. I found ways to work with my challenges instead of against them. This made a massive difference in how I thrived at work. I began to pay attention to any interrupting I might be tempted to do in meetings. I had others check my emails and other memos for clarity. I truly understood that I had not left my childhood issues behind, and I needed to build the tools to make this work for me and those around me.

Over time, I met more people who thought "differently." When I realized that others shared these distinctions, I no longer felt broken—like I needed to be fixed. Instead, I felt like more solutions were needed to make a neurodiverse workforce feel like they could succeed, again and again.

For the past twenty-five years, my own struggles— and those I witnessed in others—prompted me to create the tools you'll read about in this book. Instead of being separated from society as I once felt, I can now assimilate in my "ocean" and begin to swim a little straighter. While nothing is instantly easier, I'm equipped with the tools to educate and bring out the best in my two neurodivergent children, my neurodivergent family, and the neurodiverse employees and others I coach.

And that's why I'm passionate about this book. Not only do these stories of neurodivergence matter, but learning how to navigate potential challenges using the right strategies is crucial to the workplace, to the world, and to you.

By the way, for the purposes of learning from this book, you don't need a formal diagnosis to benefit, nor do you need to know the diagnosis of anyone around you. You simply need a desire to make the most of your environment at work and beyond.

Neurodiversity in the Workplace Today

A neurodivergent person has one or more ways in which their brain functions outside the "typical" way. For example, neurodivergent people may be diagnosed with autism, ADHD, obsessive compulsive disorder (OCD), dyspraxia, dyslexia, dyscalculia, Tourette's, or several other conditions. We will explore more terms and definitions later in this book, but for now it's important to understand that a *neurodivergent* person has brain functioning and processing that deviates from what is considered "typical." A *neurodiverse* workforce is comprised of people who have these varied conditions or syndromes, as well as those who are considered *neurotypical*.

Person-First Versus Identity-First Language

- *Person-first language* is designed to separate someone from their disability. An example of this is "person with autism."
- *Identity-first language* incorporates a person's disability into the vernacular. An example of this is "autistic person."

The general trend in medical communities has been to separate people from a disability or disease. We see this with wording like "person with Alzheimer's," "those with diabetes," and so on. Some with neurodivergence also prefer this approach and refer to themselves as a "person with autism," for example.

However, some in the autism community in particular (although this can affect other groups) prefer not to separate themselves from their diagnosis. They argue that autism is such an integral part of them that it cannot be separated from their identity; thus, they prefer to be called an "autistic person." In this book, I won't take a stand on what is right or wrong on this issue. Instead, you'll see me refer to conditions in both person-first and identity-first language. In doing so, please know that I respect each person's unique condition and challenges—as well as their right to choose their own language to discuss those things.

If you work with more than a handful of people, the odds are you work with someone who is considered neurodivergent. The brain of your coworker might not operate like everyone else's. You may even be this person yourself. How does this affect your team's projects, interactions, meetings, and goal-setting? And what can be done?

Perhaps you picked up this book because you've been diagnosed somewhere on a spectrum of neurodivergence. You may even lack a diagnosis but suspect you trend in this direction, because you typically feel like a fish lost at sea. You're tired of floating alone, but you don't even know whether to look up or down for direction.

If you're the neurodivergent "talent," you may not be gifted with millions of dollars to hire everyone to "dance around your disabilities" like some celebrities are. With no one to make up for your blunders after you put your foot in your mouth or flop in an important presentation, is there any hope for a productive work-life? You may feel ostracized or even bullied. You may miss your professional goals so regularly that failure feels like your routine. But you may still hope or wish there was something you could do to belong and succeed in a neurotypical world.

Or you may be considered neurotypical yourself, but you manage—or even love—someone with neurodivergence. If you're the employer who must oversee neurodiverse staff members who just can't seem to *get it right*, whatever that means within your team or department, you may be tempted to label them as "difficult" and coach them out the door, making them someone else's problem. But the problem is this: Even if you're weary of the frustration and high cost of turnover, if you *don't know what to do differently*, history will repeat itself the next time you hire someone with neurodivergence who just can't seem to fit in.

Perhaps you see the strengths in these employees and recognize a gap; how can you help them shine? You may be in human resources (HR), managing a university career services department, or overseeing a project team. Rather than get trapped within the cycle of frustration, disappointment, bullying, or microaggressions—involving a subtle slight, discrimination against or insult—let's say you want to change course. You care about attracting and retaining the best talent, and especially as you onboard and manage future generations, you understand that brilliance comes in many shades. You desperately need tools, but you don't know where to find them.

Whatever scenario you find yourself in, this book will provide the knowledge and resources you need to move forward. Unlike many books that focus solely on theory—explaining the myriad of ways your organization or people are malfunctioning—this one will offer pragmatic solutions to turn things around. You'll learn how those "broken" bits were meant to fit in all along, creating a whole picture that is both beautiful and functional. Instead of winging it, you will know what to do differently.

- As an *employer*, you will learn how to recruit, onboard, and retain neurodivergent employees through using the right kind of SMART goals (those that are *specific, measurable, achievable, relevant,* and *time-bound*), coaching, communications, and accommodations.

- As an *employee* with neurodivergence, you will learn simple skills that will make a massive difference, like how to network, make the most of your meetings, stay on task, engage in one-on-ones, and communicate effectively. And you will discover how to work with your manager to ensure you succeed, breaking the cycle you've been stuck in for years if not decades.

While many of the skills in this book may look familiar at first blush—because you've seen them written about in other management books—know that we're going to *flip them on their side.* By showing these concepts in a new way, this book provides practical advice for managers and employees who are navigating neurodiversity.

How do I know these strategies and tools actually work? Because I've spent decades coaching employers, employees, and students in how to implement them, and I've seen their lightbulb moments and victory laps.

As a healthcare leader for more than thirty years, I've seen individuals and organizations transformed by these simple, powerful principles.

Joan and Sam tell me these action points have helped them find their "school" in the vast sea of neurodiversity that is today's workplace, transforming their passion into purpose and, ultimately, success. I know they can help you too. So let's get swimming.

Chapter 1

EMBRACE NEURODIVERSITY IN THE WORKPLACE— DON'T MISS OUT

"Why did you do that? Are you from Mars?!"

"He sticks out like a sore thumb."

"She's a bird of a different feather."

"Don't mind Sally; that's just her way."

These phrases might be thrown out in friendly jest, but if we're honest, most of us don't relish being the "odd duck"—unless it involves holding a winning million-dollar lottery ticket. We also don't appreciate these statements, which are really microaggressions or aggressions. We may value our uniqueness, but only to a point. When our peers start thinking of our cute quirks as just plain *weird,* hearing about them on repeat starts hurting more than it humors.

As nature's most advanced herd animals, fitting in, at its core, becomes a matter of social survival. And beyond the playground, nowhere are these differences more prominently displayed—and often ridiculed or punished—than in the workplace. There, the stakes of not fitting in are unsurprisingly high. When Julie laughs inappropriately in a meeting, or Joseph can't make eye contact in interview after interview, consequences add up. HR gets involved. An organization's rare talent gets cast aside, lost in that sea of misaligned fish. I've known individuals who have ended up jobless, friendless, sometimes addicted and homeless, and worse.

But why do our differences need to be considered so strange? What if I told you a high percentage of us are actually "odd"? By odd, I mean our minds don't work like everyone else's because we are neurodivergent.

And what if I also told you that this type of oddness can be wonderful, if managed appropriately? I believe the problem isn't usually in our differences, but in how we treat them in the workplace.

If you've read the introduction, you know my family members are neurodivergent. You may now be thinking, *Of course she's going to advocate for inclusion of neurodivergence,*

BRIDGING THE GAP   19

since her own family is swimming upstream. Yes, that's true. But statistically, you'll learn that I'm not that unusual. I've discovered, from the inside out, the unique strengths and opportunities inherent in neurodivergence, even if it also brings its own challenges.

Before we dive into the "how-tos," this chapter will explore some of the context, including definitions and statistics around neurodiversity.

Neurodiversity, Neurodivergent, and Neurotypical: Odd People In

This isn't a history book, but bear with me as I divert briefly into the background and prevalence of neurodivergence, especially as it applies to the workplace.

"Neurodivergent" was first coined in the late 1990s by Judy Singer, who was born in Hungary. Singer's Jewish mother was originally sent to Auschwitz during World War II, but she was spared and allowed to work in a German airplane factory. Their family later relocated to Australia, where Singer was raised. According to a 2023 article by John Harris in *The Guardian*, Singer soon began to recognize her mother's behavior as odd. "It was like she came from another planet, or another dimension," Singer states. "She didn't understand our rules, and she would get extremely frustrated and upset.

I think I became my mother's social translator ... her naivety got her in trouble." Singer's mother would have meltdowns after she failed to pick up on social cues. She would start talking about Hungary, even if it had nothing to do with the topic at hand. While Singer recognized that some of these behaviors may have derived from her mother's past traumas, she felt there was more to those quirks.

Years later, Singer's own daughter was diagnosed with Asperger's, a high-functioning form of autism that has since been lumped into ASD. Like yours truly, Singer then recognized that her own brain also didn't operate like those around her. She began putting all the pieces together, including how her mother's behaviors might have been influenced by a unique brain.

In her forties, Singer enrolled in a university program, and in 1998, she wrote a paper titled "Odd People In"—an attempt to highlight strengths and limitations of autism while advocating for awareness to better integrate people with such differences. It was in this paper that she first used "neurodiverse," a word that might have died in obscurity had it not been for a journalist who later wrote about it.

Singer recently expressed that neurodiversity has since become a "corporate and social buzzword" that sometimes misses its main point. To some, diversity, equity, and inclusion (DEI) efforts today have become controversial. While well-intended and filling a crucial need of allowing people with differences not to be held back at work, DEI has become highly politicized, sometimes sparking rhetoric about how these programs are inefficient or unfair.

But Singer said something that captured my attention: "I'm not here to make capitalism more efficient; I'm here to make it more *humane*" (Harris 2023). Regardless of what we choose to call the act of advocating for those with disabilities or differences, I think most leaders would agree that making our workplace more "humane," as Singer stated, would be positive. And I would argue that doing so is necessary, since however we define these differences, they exist. But to take her statement further, what if we could do both—create a more *humane* workplace that is *also more efficient and profitable?* To me, that is the goal.

Today's definition of neurodiversity was adapted from Singer's original intent. While she used it to describe those with high-functioning ASD, it's now applied to anyone whose brain works differently than average.

Neurodivergent, Neurotypical, Neurodiverse

Consider these working definitions of three key terms:

- *Neurodivergent* describes a difference from the norm in cognition, sensory processing, social skills, motor skills, learning, or focus.
- The alternative—someone who is *neurotypical*—thinks or functions in a way that is considered average or normal.
- *Neurodiverse* refers to the collective differences (of both the neurodivergent and neurotypical) within a group. Our workplaces are *neurodiverse*.

We may think of ASD and ADHD as the main forms of neurodivergence, but there are many other manifestations. Some come from a medical difference, such as a distinct brain structure, genetic composition, or balance of hormones and neurotransmitters. Others are acquired as a result of injury, infection, stroke, tumor, post-traumatic stress disorder (PTSD), and so on. And others are due to other unknown factors, but they still produce behavioral changes. Consider this list of neuro-divergent conditions and traits adapted from Cleveland Clinic's website:

* Autism spectrum disorder (ASD; this includes what was once known as Asperger's syndrome)
* Attention-deficit hyperactivity disorder (ADHD) (while "attention deficit disorder (ADD)" is often used colloquially, ADHD is the correct diagnostic term)
* DiGeorge syndrome (another rare genetic disorder that affects multiple systems)
* Down syndrome
* Dyscalculia (difficulty with math)
* Dysgraphia (difficulty with writing)
* Dyslexia (difficulty with reading)
* Dyspraxia (difficulty with coordination)
* Intellectual disabilities
* Mental health conditions like bipolar disorder, obsessive-compulsive disorder (OCD), anxiety disorder, and more
* Prader-Willi syndrome (a rare genetic condition affecting metabolic, endocrine, and neurological systems)
* Sensory processing disorders

- Social anxiety (a specific type of anxiety disorder)
- Tourette syndrome
- Williams syndrome (another rare genetic disorder that affects multiple systems)

Some of these conditions may be invisible to observers, whereas others are more immediately recognizable by their traits. For the purposes of this book, it's not important to memorize or understand these conditions. Rather, recognize that neurodivergence, like candy, can come in many shapes and flavors. And it can exist on a spectrum—meaning someone may only show mild symptoms for one or more conditions, while another struggles extensively to function.

I Know What You Are, but What Am I?

"I'm so ADD."

"Blame it on my OCD."

"F***! Sorry, my Tourette's is acting up." (Okay, people might not say this, but I'm pretty sure they could!)

These have almost become catchphrases as people self-diagnose and identify based on their "quirky" behaviors. Are you easily distracted by the annoying death metal music your spouse plays while you try to pay bills at the kitchen counter? You may think you have ADD. Are you unable to sit still while paying those bills? You may call it ADHD. Do you go bonkers if your books are wonky on a shelf or pictures are askew on a wall, or when you have to touch a public doorknob? Perhaps you think it's OCD. Does this mean you should rush in for a psychiatric or medical assessment? Maybe, but not necessarily. While it's possible you have a diagnosable condition and that getting tested could help you create better accommodations and outcomes, it's also possible that even if you struggle at times, you would "pass" any tests with flying colors. Being picky about how pictures are hung doesn't affect how you get through life, but having OCD can be paralyzing. Likewise, being easily distracted doesn't automatically equate to ADD. Casual references to having these conditions minimizes the struggles of those who can't escape them.

I hope this book allows you to recognize the daily struggles of the neurodivergent and benefit from the strategies. And if you're curious about yourself, make that appointment. It can't hurt!

Now that we've defined neurodivergence, let's go back to the idea that it's "odd." According to a 2024 summary published by the Association for Career and Technical Services, research estimates that as many as 67 million people in the US fit the description of neurodivergent. When comparing this to population totals from the US Census Bureau, this means approximately one out of every five people in society—including your workplace—are considered different from the norm. If your family has more than four people, look around the dinner table; statistically, one of you is neurodivergent. Neurodivergence is hardly an anomaly.

In addition, diagnoses for neurodivergence are growing globally, largely due to better awareness and screening. While this trend is specific to children, a general rise of adult diagnoses is what's driving the societal shift, making neurodivergent conditions far more visible than ever. To me, this is a strong rationale for changing how we prepare people for the workplace. If we don't, we're bound to struggle with managing around one-fifth of our workforce. Or we may lose them altogether to attrition.

Interestingly, according to a report by the Rocky Mountain ADA Center, an even larger number of "leaders" identify as neurodivergent: 45 percent of C-level executives, 55 percent of business owners, and nearly one-third of senior management. These people aren't wallflowers or hiding under their desks. Rather they have succeeded in spite of—or perhaps because of—their conditions.

Swimming with the Sharks

I referenced sharks earlier, but maybe they aren't so scary. Afterall, three of the investment sharks from the ABC hit series *The Shark Tank* have been outspoken about their neurodivergence.

- Barbara Corcoran, the real estate mogul, speaks about how her dyslexia gave her greater resilience. Like me, she didn't recognize her own neurodivergence until her son was diagnosed.
- Kevin O'Leary also has dyslexia, which affected his reading and math skills in school. Now, he considers it a "competitive weapon."

> • Daymond John also has dyslexia.
>
> With half (a higher percentage than the general population) of the sharks sharing the same diagnosis, this reinforces the narrative that perhaps neurodivergence comes with its own leadership or entrepreneurial superpowers.

The Challenges in Neurodivergence

It's easy to recognize how someone who stands out on the playground or classroom could get bullied or dismissed. Some children are cruel, and they haven't been taught how to be kind to those who are "different." But this also happens at work, a place where people are paid to perform at the best of their abilities for the good of the organization. People gossip. Unconscious bias kicks in, and "those people" get cast aside for social lunches or overlooked in group assignments. Microaggressions fly through the air like dust particles, nearly invisible but covering everything with a thin film. Or coworkers may outright bully—gossiping or worse. None of these working conditions bring out the best performance in employees. In *The No Asshole Rule,* author Robert Sutton concludes that bullies at work cost companies twice. First, they distract the target of their bullying. That's obvious. But second, they distract and create fear in other employees who witness the bullying, fearing they will be the next target.

Unconscious Bias

As humans, many of our biased actions are triggered by automatic, subconscious thought processes. As brain scans show, even when we're not consciously choosing to judge others, our brains might be doing it. This can limit people if we treat them poorly or overlook them for promotion.

The fact that an unconscious part of ourselves might be driving the bus sounds hopeless, but it's not. Awareness is the first step toward challenging our biases. If you're interested in unraveling these biases, I encourage you to read and study more about this topic.

Even if you're in the majority and don't get picked on, these problems have consequences far beyond the neurodivergent. Here are some additional startling workplace statistics:

- "Research reveals that the unemployment rate for neurodivergent adults can be as high as 40 percent, which is about three times higher than the rate for disabled people, and nearly eight times higher than the rate for people without disabilities" (Rocky Mountain ADA Center 2024).
- Employers are "seven times more likely to recommend hiring an applicant with a physical disability (wheelchair user) than a mental illness (currently taking medication for anxiety and depression)" (Wheat et al. 2024).
- Half of neurodivergent employees report missing work due to their neurodivergence (a 5 percent increase from the previous year's survey) (Wyatt 2024).
- More than half (51 percent) of neurodivergent adults report wanting to quit their jobs due to lack of support (Christ 2023).

As a manager, you know that attrition can destroy profit and injure a culture. When you lose an employee, you must restart the recruitment process, do another round of onboarding, and conduct training all over again. Gallup has estimated the annual cost of attrition in the US at $1 trillion. When someone quits, you also lose their intellectual and social capital—which is especially harmful if they take those things to your competitor. Your tech worker or creative genius doesn't just vanish; they leave a vacuum of talent and knowledge. Especially in organizations that are changing rapidly, the employee who knows the history of your project is invaluable to you. And those with highly-specialized skillsets—like in many tech positions—can be very difficult to find. Finally, if this person contributed positively to your culture, their departure can deflate your team's engagement, which is the level of additional effort other employees are willing to invest. Recent reports by Gallup estimate that the true cost of disengagement in the US is $8.8 trillion dollars annually.

If Ravi was your star programmer, contributing to much of the innovation of your department, his loss will be felt in both measurable and immeasurable ways.

If Sierra's creativity meant the meetings she planned entertained her peers while also being informative, her loss will also be felt.

Neurodivergence can bring broader challenges, and some of the consequences are sobering. Numerous reports show that people with neurodivergence experience higher rates of anxiety, depression, and suicide. An editor friend anecdotally told me about a client she was working with on his memoir about surviving with autism in a high-tech job in Silicon Valley. Just days before his book was released, he stopped answering her emails. While he had struggled extensively with bullying at work and largely overcame it, he later died by suicide after getting sucked into a financial scam. Desperate to make up for other perceived mistakes, he got "taken" and then felt overwhelmed by his shame and embarrassment. His family was devastated, and his book that was intended to help others still hasn't been published. And somewhat ironically—given how he'd felt bullied at work most of his life—his coworkers reached out, distraught and pained by his loss.

A Special Word for College Career Advisors

If you're trying to place students in internships or jobs, everything you'll learn in this book matters and applies to you. Even if I don't address you specifically in each scenario, realize that companies will no longer seek your placements if your candidates don't succeed. This means you must know how to recognize the range of neurodiversity in your students and manage it. It also means you must equip your students—coaching them in what they can do to ensure their success, whether they are neurodivergent or going to work within a neurodiverse team. Internship programs should be set up to include training for these skills.

Finding the Strengths in Neurodivergence

Before you think of the neurodivergent as doomed or as some sort of "expendable extra" that employers are being asked to tolerate just for the sake of inclusion, think again. We, as the neurodivergent, are not blob fish to be left at the bottom of the ocean. Rather, as the *Shark Tank* example hinted at, we may be the secret ingredient to your next success. Some of the world's most brilliant and gifted people are neurodivergent, and the prevalence of this finding in our population is rising.

A Johns Hopkins University article explains how someone whose brain is "different" often comes with unique talents. They "may have a unique ability for understanding complex mathematics, recognizing obscure patterns in data, and/or memorizing intricate details. ... [They] may possess an unmatched level of concentration and a boundless imagination" ("Neuro-divergence at a Glance," October 5, 2022). In other words, someone judged as a "geek" or "nerd" may be your next superstar. They may solve your most advanced technical challenges, create a medical breakthrough, or design a user experience that seems next-level and futuristic. What leader wouldn't drool at the chance to hire the next Einstein or Steve Jobs? Even if they weren't always easy to work with, no one would dismiss their value.

Still, neurodivergent behavior often contrasts with the traits we consider as "good" in an employee. A *Harvard Business Review* article discusses how managers typically value "solid communication skills, being a team player, emotional intelligence, persuasiveness, salesperson-type personalities, the ability to network, the ability to conform to standard practices without special accommodations, and so on." While these criteria often weed out neurodivergent people, the article goes on to share how the ability to "compete on the basis of innovation has become more crucial. ... Having people who see things differently and who maybe don't fit in seamlessly 'helps offset our tendency, as a big company, to all look in the same direction,' [Silvio] Bessa [a senior vice president of digital business services at SAP] says" (Austin and

Pisano, 2017). In other words, we need these people if we want to compete. These superstars often guide the way, helping us look toward a "north star" instead of getting lost in the galaxy of typical ideas.

While I don't have access to everyone's healthcare charts to see their diagnoses, it doesn't take a medical degree to assess that many highly talented actors, singers, and athletes severely struggle with some tasks we might consider neurotypical—like staying organized and on task, showing tact in meetings, or sitting still. This is why they may have accommodations and support systems in place to ensure their success. But they also have extraordinary and irreplaceable gifts, and they often find careers to play to those strengths.

For example, Billie Eilish has been open about her Tourette syndrome, a "disorder" that hasn't stopped her from winning two Academy Awards, nine Grammy Awards, and the adoration of millions of fans. Her strengths lie in her creative genius and ability to fully immerse herself in her skills of singing and songwriting.

Additionally, many high-tech gurus who code our future gadgets are neurodivergent, which can affect how they communicate and interact with others. People like Bill Gates—who reportedly has ADHD and dyslexia— tap into investors and staff to support their inventions and dreams, filling in gaps where they can't perform. Outsourcing specific skills to others is a small price to pay for the tech empire he has built through his intellectual drive and focus, the products of which have touched nearly every person on Earth. (Afterall, I wrote this book using Microsoft Word.)

Here are more famous people who are believed to be neurodivergent. Some have been open about their diagnoses, while others—especially those who are no longer with us and may have lived before diagnoses existed—are merely speculated:

- **Steve Jobs:** Founder of Apple with dyslexia
- **Richard Branson**: Founder of the Virgin Group with dyslexia and ADHD
- **Temple Grandin:** Animal behavioralist and researcher with autism
- **Sir Anthony Hopkins:** Actor with autism
- **Tim Burton**: Filmmaker and screenwriter reported to have autism
- **Ryan Gosling:** Actor and producer with ADHD
- **Emma Watson**: Actor and UN ambassador with ADHD
- **Dan Akroyd:** Actor with Tourette syndrome

- **Daryl Hannah:** Actor with autism
- **Daniel Radcliffe**: Actor with OCD and dyspraxia
- **Simone Biles:** Olympic gymnast with ADHD
- **Michael Phelps:** Olympic swimmer with ADHD
- **David Beckham**: Legendary soccer player with OCD
- **Emily Dickenson:** Poet never diagnosed, but experts purport she may have had autism
- **Albert Einstein:** Physicist never diagnosed but purported to possibly have dyslexia, ADHD, and autism
- **Sir Isaac Newton**: Mathematician, astronomer, and physicist who is believed to have had ADHD and autism

Why Now, and Why These Tools?

I once had an employee with a tough reputation. People thought Beth wasn't very friendly, although I knew this not to be true. Let's say she had a *resting witch face*. But she was very detail-oriented. She sat quietly and could learn a claims system like no one else, finding challenges and solving them quickly. She was moved from unit to unit to troubleshoot and solve all the problems.

However, she stayed at a certain analyst level for a while. She wasn't promoted to leading a team because people perceived her as bristly. Who wants to be managed by a porcupine?

Beth was diagnosed later in life as neurodivergent. She finally understood how she was being perceived. She then learned to tell folks, "Ignore the look on my face. I'm concentrating." She set her boundaries, started working on more teams, and was coached by her manager to respond differently. Instead of saying no to something she knew the system couldn't do, she requested time to research others' questions and come back with solutions that might come close to solving their issues. Soon, she was seen as a collaborator. Eventually, she was promoted and is now an assistant director of her department. She's an example of how coaching works—not only for the employee, but for the manager who benefits from their enhanced skills.

Like Beth, I grew up before neurodivergence was widely diagnosed, although my differences presented with difficulty reading and writing as a child and through adulthood. It was only once I entered the workplace that I realized that I, too, needed to modulate my tone and facial expressions. This became even more important when my children were diagnosed with ASD and ADHD;

I needed to carefully navigate and model these important communication skills so they could make friends and thrive. Teaching them to pay attention to their tone and expressions allowed them to be better prepared for success than Beth or I had been.

Gen Xers

My generation is known for getting lost in the shuffle between the baby boomers and the millennials. We supposedly don't like to draw attention to ourselves. Many of us slipped into the front door each afternoon as latch-key kids in the 1970s through 1990s—entertaining ourselves with our Atari video games while eating a peanut butter and fluff sandwich and Cheetos (or so the stereotype goes). Perhaps that anonymity is why many of us never received a diagnosis, although I think it has more to do with the advancement in recent awareness and tools for understanding the human brain and its resulting behavior. Either way, neurodivergence is not new. It's always been there, but now we just give it a label. In my generation, we were labeled as underachievers. Anxious. Different. Only the most extreme cases were diagnosed, and the treatment and strategies were limited. This meant that many of us had to figure out how to engage with the workplace on our own, with wildly varying results. We still might not have a diagnosis, or we got one later in life. Realize this might be the employee sitting in the cubicle next to you, or it may even be you.

If we fail to hire and retain those who are neurodivergent, we're missing out on highly intelligent people—including those who could become the best engineers, programmers, planners, project managers, creative designers, and visionaries. People who struggle to perform in one area are usually phenomenal at other jobs (see more on this in chapter 2).

I know this personally. I was the director of contracting and pricing for a large company. I ran a team of twenty, kept upwards of sixty pricing jobs in my head, and organized events for my boss all the time—because those were my superpowers. Like the Tigger character in *Winnie the Pooh*, I could bounce between crises or urgent needs and address every single one of them—all before my coworkers had their morning Cheerios.

Or so it felt, being in my skin.

What others saw may have been someone with an annoying level of energy who quickly rambled off topic, interrupted inappropriately, or failed to stay on task with the mundane parts of the job. Yes, I struggled to communicate at times. I was easily distracted by details that other people could overlook like mere wallpaper in the background. My ADHD-influenced brain could rightfully be seen as a liability, but I was lucky to have a boss who saw it as an asset. "There's nobody who puts out a dumpster fire better than you," he told me regularly.

Once I recognized my condition, this didn't mean I could dismiss all my weaknesses and blame them on neurodivergence; I was still responsible enough to address and curtail any weaknesses that were tripping me up. So I learned to create the organizational tools necessary for success, first as an individual contributor in the corporate world. As I moved into leadership roles, I added tools to help me build and manage teams. These strategies helped me as a leader in hospitals, consulting firms, and medical device companies.

The most important of these tools—which you'll learn much more about throughout this book—involved mentoring and coaching my team to meet challenges. I helped them through situations like those I had faced when entering the workforce. I helped the neurotypical and the neurodivergent. This included helping a neurotypical employee cope with a neurodiverse manager.

Even as corporations are retreating from DEI, these tools matter to organizations because:

- The neurodivergent represent some of your greatest talent. This talent is hard to find and expensive to replace. You therefore need to cultivate talent wherever you find it (looking in places others may not).
- Almost all the techniques we discuss in this book will help both neurodivergent and neurotypicals alike. If you apply these lessons to your team as a whole, you will benefit the entire team.
- Effectively managing your neurodiverse team is likely to increase your company's return on investment while decreasing turnover.

Invisible Disabilities Deserve Recognition

When someone breaks their leg and walks with crutches, we immediately move to open the door for them. We have no problem making accommodations so they can do their work, because we understand their value hasn't changed. Similarly, if someone is bound to a wheelchair for life, we usually see their limitations *and* their value, and we can clearly find ways to make their work-life more productive and easier. It's no different for many who are neurodivergent, except that, like with conditions such as diabetes or dysautonomia, we can't always *see* their disability or challenges. That's why it's important to foster a workplace that is equipped to thrive with neurodiversity.

Once again, let me reinforce that one in five people you work with is neurodivergent. That's a lot! This means:

- If you're a manager or supervisor, 20 percent of the people you're responsible and accountable for are neurodivergent.
- If you're in sales, 20 percent of your customers are neurodivergent. While the techniques and strategies that you use with customers will differ somewhat, you need to be mindful when you engage with them.

- If you're an individual contributor, 20 percent of your coworkers are neurodivergent—a statistic that includes your manager.
- At least 20 percent of the people reading this are neurodivergent, and many of you may not have been formally diagnosed yet.

While we might think of the neurotypical as "normal" and the neurodivergent as "abnormal," the reality is that a normal society includes great neurodiversity. Like in a tapestry of many colors, every thread is relevant and needed. They all create the garment that allows our society and workplaces to function.

Throughout this book, we will explore more about the strengths and challenges of a neurodiverse workforce. But more importantly, you will learn what you can do to maximize these differences, even if you're not a celebrity or multi-millionaire. These strategies apply from recruitment to onboarding, and they also work in helping you or your employee to get a promotion.

- As a *manager*, you will discover strategies for recruiting and retaining neurodiverse employees—while minimizing frustration and maximizing their performance and engagement. This includes the

unique challenges of generation Z, which will be
replaced by new challenges from the generation
behind them as the pattern of needing to adapt
to changes repeats itself.

◆ As an *employee*, you will learn how to tap into your
strengths, keep your weaknesses from tripping
you up, and thrive on your team—even if you
feel like a square peg in a round hole.

These are skills that also should be taught in any college
or university because they are critical to functioning in
the workplace and understanding our fellow humans.

No matter your role, age, and diagnosis (or lack
thereof), you need to be equipped with the specific leadership skills necessary to thrive in today's increasingly
neurodiverse world. While these skills apply no matter
how your brain operates, they are even more crucial if
you're neurodivergent or work with someone who is.

Chapter 2

MAXIMIZE PEOPLE AT WORK—NAVIGATE SKILLS, STRENGTHS, AND WEAKNESSES

The phrase "what's good for the goose is good for the gander" functions beyond the farmyard. While the neurodivergent can benefit from specific strategies to optimize their performance, a few skills are critical for *everyone* in the workplace. They form the foundation upon which everything else is built. We'll explore these concepts and their application to both managers and employees.

- If you're a *manager*, these principles and skills— often associated with being a strong leader—are foundational, regardless of the unique composition of your employees' brains. These are the skills that have proven to foster employee retention and satisfaction.

- If you're an *employee* with no formal leadership role, these concepts will help you develop your own skills so you can become indispensable at work. By teaching critical thinking and clear communication, if you aspire to lead others in the future, these skills are crucial to be successful in your role.

It's often easier to learn why skills are critical by studying those who lack them, namely bad bosses or a poor teammate. If you've held a job, you've probably encountered one of these. Maybe you've even been this boss or teammate at times. (I have, before I learned to do better.)

Could you describe how a "bad boss" acts at work? When I ask this question of most coaching clients, I get answers like:

- "She micromanages the living daylights out of everything I do—breathing down my neck—and doesn't trust anyone. Then when I do something great, she ignores it."
- "He yells at his staff like we aren't even human."

- "I have no clue what I'm supposed to be doing, because their communication is so bad."
- "I go to work afraid I'll get it wrong, or worse, lose my job."

Traditional "Theory X" management style was developed by a professor at the Massachusetts Institute of Technology, Sloan School of Management, Douglas McGregor, in the 1950s and further refined in the 1960s. It saw employees as components in a machine that must be forced to do their jobs, with little need for context or motivation. In this management style, leaders valued compliance over creativity, disciplining any employee who "got out of line." It assumes that employees are unmotivated and must be pushed to do their jobs. You can probably see why this management style would be problematic in a neurodiverse workforce, since everyone who doesn't fit into a rigid standard may end up disciplined, or even let go.

In contrast, McGregor's "Theory Y" management style assumes people want to do well, and that they can be intrinsically motivated. Many of today's best Theory Y leaders encourage employees to "color outside of the lines" when their role warrants it. These leaders know that the Theory X management style is outdated.

So how can we implement those Theory Y practices? It starts with recognizing someone for who they are, including their unique strengths.

Strengths-Based Leadership

In Chapter 1, we explored unique challenges and strengths of the neurodivergent. If you're neurodivergent, you know your challenges because they hit you in the head every day. Even if you lack awareness of them, someone else is bound to tell you something like, "You talk too much," "Why can't you pay attention?" "You don't make any sense when you speak!" "Could you *please* make eye contact for once?" "You're so weird!" You probably also know some of your own gifts—the ones you wish others would see as more colorful than your weaknesses. Maybe your boss recognizes the real you, but if you're like many employees, you struggle to feel appreciated—or even accepted.

Dr. David Rendall jokes from the stage about how in his relationship, deodorant is more important than breath mints, since he is 6 feet, 6 inches, and his wife is 4 feet, 10 inches. But his differences extend beyond height. As a child, he aggravated his teachers. He couldn't sit still. He talked excessively in class. He played pranks that got his classmates laughing while distracting them from their lessons. Fast forward several decades, and he's now a professional speaker. He entertains and educates thousands on stage every year—all around the world—doing the very things his teachers once labeled as deviant: talking a lot, moving around frenetically as he paces onstage, and delivering jokes and motivation with impeccable timing. Just like the celebrities featured in the last chapter, David found the assets embedded in his challenging behaviors. His often unusual— and always funny—twist on how he sees the world is his strength.

That sounds great for people like him, you might be thinking. *But what about us 'regular folk' who aren't winning a Grammy, gracing a keynote stage, or experiencing an IPO of our own company—and who don't expect those things anytime soon? How do we uncover our strengths at work, and why does this process matter?*

Similarly, our friends have a child who used to take apart their electronics or rewire items in their home to make other things and see how they worked. Now he's an adult, and without having finished college, he's an IT consultant who fixes issues for large companies. This child could not sit still in class or focus on finishing assignments, but if you placed him in front of a computer, he could solve the world's problems.

These people are not only Grammy winners or chief executive officers (CEOs); they include our everyday workers in our companies.

There's a field of research behind why focusing on strengths works. Martin Seligman, PhD, started the strengths movement in the 1990s, and today he's known as the leading pioneer in the field of positive psychology. Instead of studying what made people broken, Seligman researched what brought them success. He leveraged from earlier work by Abraham Maslow on studying humans' strength and potential rather than their neuroses. Seligman first studied dogs and how their learned helplessness would limit their behavior. Soon, he transferred this research to humans.

Learned Helplessness

Learned helplessness is when we give up on trying to help ourselves because we've come to believe that doing so is futile. This may be due to past experience or trauma. For example, someone with neurodivergence might believe they can't hold a job because they haven't yet found a workplace that accommodates them and allows their mind to flourish.

The results of Seligman's work were groundbreaking. As he stated at the Lincoln Summit on September 28, 1999, "The most important thing we learned was that psychology was half-baked. We've baked the part about mental illness, about repair damage. The other side's unbaked, the side of strength, the side of what we're good at."

The work of Don Clifton complemented these ideas. Clifton originally served in World War II before returning to study at the University of Nebraska-Lincoln in 1949. Eventually, this led him to start the Nebraska Human Resources Research Foundation with colleagues. He began teaching educational psychology, and he noticed how students who graduated had different character traits than those who failed to finish their degrees. "What would happen if we studied what was *right* with people versus what's wrong with people?» he wondered (Gallup.com).

Eventually, he founded a consultancy that later merged with Gallup, the renowned polling organization and world leader in employee engagement and leadership. There, he created tools to help employers identify top performers in different jobs. While this helped organizations, it didn't always help those individuals. So in the mid-1990s, he expanded on this research—creating an assessment to identify specific traits that could help an individual better understand and develop themselves. "Clifton establishes the powerful premise on which the CliftonStrengths movement would grow: Companies, leaders, and those they lead can achieve more by focusing on strengths rather than only on weaknesses" (Gallup.com).

In 2001, Clifton partnered with Marcus Buckingham to produce the book *Now Discover Your Strengths*, sold with an online assessment. Designed for the digital age, this brought strengths-based leadership content to the masses. Clifton's grandson Tom Rath later contributed to the field, and in 2006, the tool was revised using psychometrics. Today, millions of people have taken this assessment, and the updated book, *StrengthsFinders 2.0*, is listed by Gallup as the bestselling business book of all time and Amazon's top nonfiction seller.

One of the most important tenets of strengths-based leadership is that we don't want a team made up of all the same strengths. How fun would that be? But enjoyment aside, it wouldn't be useful. The best teams are often formed of individuals who bring different strengths to the team. Think of this like operating an airplane. We need mechanics to tune it up and check that the wheels are going to stay intact, pilots to navigate it, and flight attendants to engage passengers who need a drink, diaper, or place to put their lumpy suitcase. Each of these roles requires different skills, but collectively they're helping a plane-full of people reach Cancun or wherever their heart desires. The last thing passengers want is a team of airline personnel trying to wrestle the yoke out of the pilot's hands!

Gallup's StrengthsFinder assessment lists thirty-four strengths. I'm listing them below, but I know they may seem abstract at first glance. If you want to know more about them, check out the StrengthsFinder resource for full definitions and consider taking the assessment yourself or a similar one.

1. Achiever	2. Activator	3. Adaptability	4. Analytical
5. Arranger	6. Belief	7. Command	8. Communication
9. Competition	10. Connectedness	11. Consistency	12. Context
13. Deliberative	14. Developer	15. Discipline	16. Empathy
17. Focus	18. Futuristic	19. Harmony	20. Ideation
21. Includer	22. Individualization	23. Input	24. Intellection
25. Learner	26. Maximizer	27. Positivity	28. Relator
29. Responsibility	30. Restorative	31. Self-Assurance	32. Significance
33. Strategic	34. Woo (winning others over)		

You might be surprised that some strengths could come across as negative in some contexts. Has anyone told you to be less *competitive* or that you're *too positive?* You aren't alone. While any strength, when taken to an extreme, could cause harm, it can also be highly beneficial when harnessed and put to good use. Consider a salesperson who must make endless cold calls; they need to be both positive and competitive!

As introduced in the last chapter, we aren't great at recognizing how differences in others can benefit us all. Our competitive nature—the one we all have to some degree, regardless of our strengths—often dominates. We may even try to make everyone "like us" to make our job easier—or so we think.

A colleague recently told me about her work consulting a hospice organization with her partner. The leaders hoped to position themselves for a merger, but to do so, they needed to improve their operations. With a mission focused on caring well for their patients, they often neglected critical details of running the company. Meanwhile, in individual coaching sessions with the managers, the consultants heard many complaints about their chief financial officer (CFO). These leaders confided something like, "Jasmine is so anal retentive. All she cares about is compliance and money." Their faces scoffed as they spoke of these "annoying" traits. (Hopefully you see the irony here.)

These managers soon met for a workshop where they discussed the results of their individual strengths assessments. The team was surprised at their outcomes, but the consultants weren't. Nearly all of them had top strengths like "empathy," "connection," and "belief." Guess who was the only one with "futuristic," "winning others over," and "strategic" strengths?" You guessed it: the CFO. The managers had an aha moment as they realized why Jasmine's strengths were so valuable to their goal of not only providing the best service but also attracting a merger partner. Afterall, they needed to prepare for the *future* and *woo* a partner while being *strategic* about where they spent their money. More importantly, Jasmine's teammates started treating her differently. Jasmine felt better too because she no longer was ostracized for doing her job well.

Also of note, no one on this team had strengths like "achiever" or "action"—the type that would lead to *getting stuff done*. But guess who did? The consultants. This management team knew they needed to make their goal actionable, and the consultants could help round out their team's strengths to make this happen. A few years later, the organization achieved the merger.

If they'd failed to lean into their diverse strengths, this beloved community hospice might have folded—which would have been tragic for the families who depended on it to compassionately guide them through their most challenging losses.

- ✦ As you identify your individual strengths, recognize that somewhere, a team needs your gifts.
- ✦ And if you're managing others, consider how the diverse strengths of your team can complete the masterpiece you're desiring. Build your team to work together and appreciate each other's strengths.

Gallup shares that the possible combinations of strengths are so unique that "the chance of you sharing the same top five CliftonStrengths themes in the same order with another person is one in 33 million" (Bailey, 2024). Do you feel *different*? Great! The world needs someone just like you.

More Than Meets the Eye

When it comes to understanding the neurodivergent, most people picture characters from *Rain*

Man, The Good Doctor, Atypical, or something they've seen on TV or a news story of someone dangerous who has ASD. To paraphrase the Broadway play featuring neurodivergent actors, *How to Dance in Ohio,* if you have met one neurodivergent person, you have met one neurodivergent person. We are all different. And we all have unique strengths.

We've established that diverse strengths are critical to a team. But what about *weaknesses?* Do they matter at all?

There's a reason the StrengthsFinder assessment was only designed to provide each participant's top five strengths. The philosophy is that you'll be more successful if you maximize strengths rather than trying in vain to "fix" weaknesses. Research suggests:

- People already know and have been told repeatedly about their weaknesses in hopes they'll overcome them, and
- Focusing on strengths can minimize people's weaknesses.

By focusing on strengths, the assessment prevents you from focusing on the least important information—your weaknesses. Even if you can't resist the temptation and skip to the bottom of your list of five traits, you'll still be focused on a strength.

While you can move the needle on your strengths through training or practicing a skill, you're probably inclined toward certain tasks or roles. If naturally drawn to "connect" with people, for example, you may feel stir-crazy and miserable while isolated in a basement cubicle.

Dance with the Stars—But Only at Home

To understand "weaknesses," consider the skill of dancing. With two left feet, you could watch "Dancing with the Stars" for hours and still terrify your cat as you attempt to mimic the experts' dazzling moves in your living room. You could even sign up for classes, but you'd likely still never get recruited for a Broadway show. That doesn't mean you can't learn to dance better; you just might never be great—which is okay. You'll just dance less poorly. Find what you're naturally inclined to do, and become superb at it!

While I believe that strengths should be your focus, weaknesses merit discussion too.

First, don't use weaknesses as an excuse for poor behavior. If an employee's weakness is so glaring that it distracts or inhibits a colleague's performance, then it's a problem. If an employee is behaving like a jerk, they've got to fix it. If they're inhibiting productivity or simply not getting their work done, address the problem; don't make excuses. Strengths-based leadership can guide people into the right roles and maximize their engagement, but we're all still held to consistent standards based on our organization's mission statement, values, guiding principles, and goals. If one of those values is integrity, for example, illegally shredding financial documents due to a lack of understanding them is no excuse. We must find someone with those critical strengths and skills and put people where they can shine.

Spotlighting Your Weaknesses

Dr. David Rendall, author of *The Freak Factor*, also shares a somewhat contrarian approach to weaknesses— believing they can provide clues to our strengths. "What makes you weird makes you wonderful," he states in his speeches, encouraging audiences to amplify their weaknesses and even leverage a career from them.

Consider how Jasmine's "anal-retentive" ways improved the hospice's bottom line and attracted a merger partner. Or how Rendall amplified his weakness of "talking too much" by becoming a professional speaker.

What are your "weaknesses?" What do others say when they complain about—or needle—you? Maybe you hear:

+ "You're so 'out there' with your ideas." *Could you be well-suited in a creative role where you can imagine new solutions?*
+ "You're so serious, always focused on the minutiae." *Could a role in finance, project management, IT, or operations be ideal for you?*

Are You a Closet Writer?

An executive I know was asked by his boss to draft the introduction to a book that would be given to all employees in the company. While his boss hadn't authored the book, the publisher offered this customized introduction to personalize it for their organization. After the boss read this ghost-written draft of the introduction, he told my friend, "Are you sure you're not a frustrated writer hiding in our company? Because what you wrote is phe-nomenal. I wouldn't change a word. Please send it to the publisher." My friend later left his corporate job, and today he's a best-selling author and professional ghostwriter. And by the way, he has dyslexia—thinking in stories rather than spread-sheets and data.

If you're neurodivergent, I believe you have super-powers embedded in your diagnosis. Instead of being successful *in spite of* having ADHD or ASD, what if you could also excel *because of* some of the strengths it grants you? Look back over the list of celebrities in Chapter 1 and note how many of them have become superstars due to their strength in technical, creative, or entrepre-neurial pursuits, for example. The distracted class clown can become a skilled comedian or public speaker. The kid that takes apart the vacuum may become an engineer and inventor.

Realize that I don't intend to dismiss the vast chal-lenges inherent in being neurodivergent. You may feel like you're in a never-ending battle to advocate for yourself and be understood at school, work, and beyond. Getting through the day—something that your peers seem to do with ease—may feel like it takes all your effort. And your relationships may feel strained and challenged. But with the right help and systems in place—and by learning how to utilize these strategies—it can be like a superpower, propelling you to great things.

If you're neurodivergent, you already know how much you struggle, and I empathize; after all, that's why I wrote this book. You've probably been working twice as hard as others to get where you are. While you've been working to discover your strengths, everyone else has only pointed out your weaknesses. While I see you in this pain, I'm also encouraging you to *flip your diagnosis on its side* and find your inherent strengths.

- As an *employee*, ask yourself if there's an embedded clue within your weaknesses that might help you excel in a different role—or a different task within your current role.
- If you're *managing others*, a focus on strengths—and possibly weaknesses—may cause you to move an employee into a different role to maximize what they're actually great at.

This is the type of issue I tackle with clients in my coaching work, so don't be afraid to seek help from someone objective to help you navigate and find your best role.

Strengths-based leadership is not only crucial to consider as you manage others (or yourself), but it's especially applicable in a neurodiverse workforce. To maximize performance, you must see people for who they are—including what makes them strong. I challenge you to recognize that these differences come with embedded assets.

Chapter 3

RECRUIT FOR THE NEURODIVERSE— TALENT IS DISTRIBUTED EQUALLY; OPPORTUNITY IS NOT

Whether you're a manager or employee, this concept is key: Engage with your colleagues like they matter. As the famous quote states, "Be kind, for everyone you know is fighting a hard battle" (attributed in various forms to several people, including Plato). Kindness and respect start during recruitment, which is the first touchpoint between a potential employer and employee.

There are many steps in the recruitment process. As a manager, your first step is to answer: What are the skills you need to hire for in your team? Do you need an analyst, a programmer, or an admin? In the book *Good to Great*, author Jim Collins talks about getting the right people on the bus. I can hire people to take the bus where I'm going today, or I can hire people who can adapt if the direction needs to change tomorrow. Nobody wants to need to fire their team if the direction changes. Instead, as you get the right people on the bus, choose those who will still be able to keep you moving forward even as you pivot to a new direction.

To select people who can stay on the bus for longer, consider: What is the job description you need to fill, and what are the minimum skills you can accept? Then write your description to include someone who may exceed those standards. You want to avoid having to rewrite and repost the job later if a great candidate walks through the door.

As you draft the job posting, also make sure it's very clearly written so that any candidate will understand what you're seeking. Future employees who are neuro-divergent are often very literal and may not apply if the job description is ambiguous.

Where you recruit your talent is also important. Some sites will focus on recruiting for the neurodiver-gent and help them through the interview process. You can work directly with college career centers and job fairs. You can also seek out specialists to help you build programs to hire neurodiverse candidates.

One place where you can lose a great candidate is in the resume review process.

AI, Technology Tools, and Recruiting: Navigating the Wild West

Depending on who you talk to, artificial intelligence (AI) is either the biggest opportunity or the gravest threat to humanity. In the recruitment of employees, this dichotomy is no different.

As an employer, on one hand, AI allows you to sift through thousands of job applications using filters to target what you most need. As an employee, it allows you to find job listings that match your specific desires and network with hiring managers without ever setting foot in the same room. And once at work, tech tools like Zoom, Slack, and the new ones being released daily can improve productivity and allow work to happen from anywhere, at any time.

These improved online communication and project management tools offer many benefits for the neurodivergent. For example, those who work best in a quiet space may be granted work-from-home opportunities to maximize their performance.

But we also find challenges with this technology.

One of the gravest issues I see when embedding AI into the recruiting process is the filtering out of employees who may be the best for certain roles. When a company is using AI to analyze resumes, that software is "trained" for a specific "norm"—meaning it's programmed to pick out the resumes that most align with whatever it's told to look for. Suppose a neurodivergent candidate doesn't write their cover letter and resume to that norm. The hiring manager may miss that star engineer who could catapult their company to the next level or the highly creative marketing associate who would rock the next product launch on social media. When an AI filter is applied, those superstar performers we learned about in the past two chapters might become invisible. Imagine missing a Bill Gates or Barbara Corcoran—cast aside, never to even be interviewed.

If you use AI recruitment tools, you must ensure that the software is trained to factors that are your most meaningful indicators of success, while eliminating as many biases as possible that may filter out the neurodivergent. Test the system with the resumes of your current employees and see who is recommended versus filtered out. If your AI recruiter is filtering out people who are your current above-average performers, you need to reevaluate the tool and how it was implemented. You can't afford to miss this talent.

When a resume passes the initial screening, the next phase of the recruitment often involves an automated screening process that may include games, timed Excel tests, and experiential questions. Since some people with autism or ADHD also have anxiety, a timed test could automatically exclude them from the next section of the interview process. If these neurodivergent candidates see a timer counting down and become anxious and therefore unable to function, these new interview processes may eliminate some top candidates.

Even if a candidate makes it past the first two rounds of AI filtering and gets their resume accepted, many first-round interview practices have become so automated that they're counterproductive. When we think of an "interview," we imagine two-way communication. But today, many screening interviews are done using a video recording or chat bot, which hardly feels *human*.

In these video recordings, a candidate logs onto a screen, is given a prompt, and within a set amount of time, must spontaneously answer a question—all while on video. I'll confess that this type of interview would absolutely paralyze me! I tend to ramble as I speak, especially if I'm nervous or enthusiastic about a topic. Again, anyone with anxiety around time limits may see the clock ticking down and fumble with their words or say something that later keeps them up at night, kicking themselves as they count sheep.

With security concerns around AI becoming a bigger issue, some employees are also feeling apprehensive about recording their audio and video for an unknown company or recruiter to access and use at their discretion. Companies must be aware of these security risks and potential violations to candidates' welfare.

Chatbot interviews bring additional challenges. Think about your last customer service AI interaction, perhaps for the non-functioning microwave you bought on Amazon. This "chat" puts you into a continuous loop and, if the session is particularly bad, it ends only in cursing and muttering about how "it's a good thing that the chatbot lives in the cloud." AI-based interviews may work fine for standard questions of people who fall within the norm, but with a neurodivergent workforce, too many nuances get missed. If a candidate answers in an unconventional way, the AI will likely miss their actual meaning. This becomes problematic, especially when responding to some of the deeper, more intelligent questions a potential employer or employee may ask.

In summary, something is lost in the interviewing process when a human is taken out of the mix. As one candidate stated, "I would be much more likely to join an organization if I could speak to the hiring manager and ask questions about the culture. Even if that chatbot is amazing and I can't necessarily differentiate between it and a person, there is something to be said for still having the human touch" (Heinze, 2023).

Leaning into Neurodiverse Hiring

Despite ongoing changes, some companies are still taking extra steps to ensure they properly recruit and equip a neurodiverse workforce by providing a separate process or program for neurodivergent internships, hiring, and onboarding.

Dell states on their website: "We provide a skill-based interview experience designed to include all learning and communication styles. Through a neurodivergent-friendly recruitment process, we aim to provide all job seekers with support resources that promote success from application to onboarding, including interview preparation support, mentoring and coaching and professional development." As a result of this and their Autism Hiring Program of 2018, managers "describe a more close-knit, focused team of employees with autistic workers introducing new problem-solving methods" (Miller, 2023). Other companies with unique neurodiversity hiring programs include:

- SAP—a German software company—claims to have a 90 percent retention rate amongst the neurodivergent (Birch, 2021).
- Microsoft's Neurodiversity Hiring Program is based on "the belief that neurodivergent individuals strengthen a workforce with innovative thinking and creative solutions" (Microsoft.com).
- JP Morgan, the banking firm, offers an internship that identifies and fosters non-verbal and autistic talent while at the university level.
- Ford Motor Company has a program for autistic people as well as for those with mental and physical disabilities.
- Google Cloud works in conjunction with the Stanford Neurodiversity Project to enhance its neurodiverse hiring and management.

These companies recognize the unique skills inherent in neurodivergence, including ASD. They are combating the statistics, which show that only 15 to 20 percent of adults with ASD are employed full-time, contrasted to 60 to 70 percent of neurotypical people (NeuroLaunch.com, 2024).

However, even in companies that state they have these programs, they may not be consistently implemented across all of their teams. And as I write this, many DEI programs are being dismantled in US organizations, so the future of these neurodivergent hiring programs is unknown.

I'm not naïve or old fashioned enough to think AI tools will—or even should—go away. But I think it's important to know the limitations they place on recruiting, so we can identify some crucial modifications and accommodations. If you're an employer looking to hire someone, consider these strategies, which apply particularly to a neurodiverse workforce:

- **Provide alternative methods for candidates to interview whenever possible.** Err on the side of treating people like individuals. Of course, human interviewers have bias too, but with training, they can learn to recognize neuro-divergent talent. How would each of your family members interview best based on their learning styles and potential neurodiversity? Offer as many of these options as possible.

◆ **Consider the strengths and skills needed for the job, and don't expect every candidate to shine in the recruiting process.** Hiring a tech worker? Maybe they don't need to present well on screen if they have a solid track record and can communicate effectively to team members. Can you give them an alternate method of assessing their skills, such as solving a real problem?

▫ I recently heard about the software company, Red Hat, interviewing an employee, Amida, for a business analyst role, only to learn that she hadn't memorized many of the key terms associated with the software they used to process data. "I know how to do this stuff in my sleep," Amida told the hiring manager. "I just don't know how to explain it." Instead of dismissing Amida because she didn't check all the boxes in the interview, they were innovative enough to give her another option; they left her in a room with a complex, real problem their team was working on. After a short while, Amida solved their problem—better than anyone on the team had yet done. She was hired on the spot. And by the way, Amida had ADD. Her condition also had caused her to struggle to complete her college degree, but she had no problem performing well on the job. Red Hat was also innovative enough to overlook her lack of degree on her resume and offer her a chance (something that AI filters might not allow).

- **Don't be immediately alarmed by a lack of eye contact.** Some of the most creative or talented people with neurodivergence find it almost impossible to retain direct eye contact. Again, is maintaining it necessary to the role? If not, consider overlooking this trait. If you're someone who struggles with eye contact, you may not have a manager who "gets" this, since it's typically an expected behavior in Western society. It's therefore important to find ways to show that you're paying attention (because you are!) even if you can't hold eye contact.

  - One strategy I recommend to my clients is to take notes while the other person is talking, looking up briefly here and there. This allows your eyes to go somewhere else while showing that you value what the person is saying enough to document it. This works in interviews but also while on the job in meetings or one-on-one feedback sessions. Carrying a small notebook with you—perhaps with your own pre-written notes and questions—allows you to access this tool readily.

- If you're on screen, try looking into the camera (not the person's eyes), or off to the side slightly. Or position your computer screen so that something appears behind it—maybe a wall with a picture on it, or a window you can look out. One person I know puts Post-Its on the wall with encouraging statements like, "You've got this!" You can then move your gaze between these spots and still look like you're engaged with the person on screen.

- If that still feels like too much stimulation, you can often minimize or even hide the view of the video on your screen while still looking at your computer. Unless the person is showing you something important like a document, they likely won't know you aren't looking at them. Just remember to smile periodically to show your human side!

- **Constantly reassess your recruiting sources.** Since AI may be filtering out some of the best talent or those with the strengths you need, consider joining associations or groups where you can meet other viable candidates in person. For entry-level positions or those that require a specific skill set, reach out to universities or tech schools for their recommendations. You won't find a shortcut for these one-on-one human interactions. Building strategic relationships like this will pay off long-term when you become the go-to source for placing their talented candidates.

- **Offer more internships.** If it seems too risky to hire someone full-time, consider coops or paid internships for a "rent before you buy" option. You will have to onboard and mentor someone in the process, but you will benefit from their fresh-out-of-school knowledge and curiosity while you share your knowledge and experience. And you may end up discovering a hidden talent before your competition does.

Digging Deeper to Understand a Candidate

At one point in my career, I had a dilemma in choosing which of two candidates to hire.

Everyone really liked the first candidate. In fact, my boss thought they were perfect. This person was very friendly and outgoing, but I didn't think they could do the job as well as the second candidate. And when I checked this "perfect" candidate's references, I learned they didn't get along well with either of their prior female bosses.

My second candidate had a quiet demeanor. He also didn't get along with his previous manager, and he was very analytical. He was different from the rest of the team, but he was what I thought I needed in terms of his strengths and skills. Also, he came with a solid reference from HR—offering what I saw as a good balance of talent and ability to work within a team.

I went to bat and hired the second candidate. He turned out to be great in his role, as he uncovered all the issues I needed to be found with

our contracts. He was definitely not a candidate
I would have wanted to miss out on.

Recruiting, when done well, is like matchmaking.
The hope is that it will turn into a long-term relationship, or at a minimum, one that is mutually beneficial
for both parties. But before it can be done, those parties
must find each other.

Chapter 4

EQUIP NEURODIVERSE GRADUATES FOR THEIR INTERNSHIP OR FIRST ROLE

A Special Note for University Career Advisors and Managers

Let me be direct: Many universities are failing students, and especially the neurodivergent. I don't mean in the classroom. I mean in providing them a safe and consistent bridge to the workplace. (And no, not all of them are failing, but enough that I feel I must say this.) To resolve this, I believe a university's career services department must look for ways to move their services into the classroom so that students don't need to struggle to find these solutions.

A recent article in *Harvard Business Review* backs this up by sharing about a study of Americans who had graduated from a two-year/community or four-year college in the past five years. "Nearly one in five (19 percent) reported that their college education experience did not provide them with the skills needed to perform their first post-degree job. Additionally, more than half (53 percent) of these college graduates have not applied to an entry-level job in their field because they felt unqualified, and nearly half (42 percent) felt unqualified because they did not have all the skills listed in the job description" (Hansen, 2021).

In my management and coaching work, I've seen so many fresh-out-of-college interns or employees ill-equipped to handle even basic communications and processes required to do a job. This frustrates managers, and it creates problems for the universities if their internships don't show efficacy in creating longer-term job opportunities.

In 2024, the National Association of Colleges and Employers (NACE) conducted a survey of employers regarding what skills they saw as key for graduates arriving to their workplaces. Similarly, they were asked what skills they saw as missing in this same group.

* These employers reported their top three necessary competencies as *communication, critical thinking*, and *teamwork*. They indicated that students were only somewhat proficient in these.
* The same employers then rated the top competencies that graduates were actually showing up with. *Teamwork* was number one. However, *technology* as well as *equity and inclusion* took the other two top spots (Gatta et al., 2024)—with *communications* and *critical thinking* falling low on the list of competencies held.

Employers Rate the Importance of the Career-Readiness Competencies	
Competencies:	Weighted Average Rating:
Communication	4.57
Critical Thinking	4.49
Teamwork	4.43
Professionalism	4.31
Equity and Inclusion	3.98
Technology	3.93
Career and Self-Development	3.81
Leadership	3.53
5-point scale where 1=Not at all proficient, 2=Not very proficient, 3=Somewhat proficient, 4=Very proficient, and 5=Extremely proficient	

Employers Rate Recent Graduates on the Eight Career-Readiness Competencies	
Competencies:	Weighted Average Rating:
Teamwork	4.00
Technology	3.91
Equity and Inclusion	3.78
Critical Thinking	3.67
Communication	3.62
Professionalism	3.50
Career and Self-Development	3.43
Leadership	3.21
5-point scale where 1=Not at all proficient, 2=Not very proficient, 3=Somewhat proficient, 4=Very proficient, and 5=Extremely proficient	

Tables recreated from Job Outlook 2025 with the permission of the National Association of Colleges and Employers, copyright holder.

This reflects a gap between what employers want and what graduates have been prepared to offer, which suggests that higher education is not providing students with the skills that employers value. Colleges have seemingly emphasized proficiency with technology tools, which are constantly evolving, at the expense of communication and critical thinking skills, whose value will only grow over time.

This trend also plays out in the hiring process itself. I have attended several webinars at NACE recently regarding students' career readiness, and the focus has continued to be on the resume building, LinkedIn posting, and interview process. They have meanwhile downplayed the importance of other critical career readiness skills.

While there's been a push to increase career readiness and bring it into the classroom, key gaps are still being ignored. Instead of diving into this need and developing the critical skills that employers want, career services groups are often utilizing AI to assist with resumes, cover letters, mock interviews, and salary negotiation. Once again, AI does not have the ability to consider students who are neurodivergent. Those who might have a flat affect or be monotone, or those with Tourette's or ADHD, will not be well coached by an AI coach. And working with AI won't actually help them with real-life communication.

Closing this gap takes time and commitment by both the university career officer and the corporate sponsors of internship programs. Following are some solutions that start in the university and extend into the corporate setting.

Solution #1: Integrate Teaching of Critical Skills into the Core College or University Curriculum Prior to Internships

Any of the basic skills that are trained within the workplace should be given to students before they even look for jobs. These skills need to be included in the classwork and modeled in how the student is taught in college. Many of these skills are important for project-based learning and other group assignments.

For example, universities should teach students to come up not only with key questions, but with possible solutions to those issues. Then real problem-solving skills can be reinforced in the classwork that is assigned by the professor. This classwork may include addressing a real-world problem sponsored by an employer, which allows students to do real research. While engaging in this problem-solving, students get a chance to begin working as a team, practice one-on-ones with a manager or professor, and create a final presentation.

This approach will help students gain some of the skills while giving neurodivergent students a safe place to practice before moving out to the workplace. It would allow them to receive feedback on their skillset as well.

Skills that should be taught before students graduate include:

* Critical thinking
* Meeting etiquette
* Basic communication skills using different mediums such as group messaging (Slack, Teams), email, telephone (audio only), web meetings (audio and video), and face-to-face, including when and how to use each medium
* "Corporate speak"—what certain terms mean and what to expect in a corporate setting
* How to ask *quality* questions to get the right answers
* How to conduct basic research on various topics to expand skills
* How to research a prospective employer (what products and services they provide, what their vision and mission are) and/or hiring manager (current role, educational background, prior roles, and so on)
* How to advocate for oneself to get help—from peers, managers, and HR if needed

Solution #2: Equip Managers and Supervisors Up Front with the Skills and Tools to Support Neurodivergent Interns and Employees

This is a bigger-than-a-breadbox "ask," but if you're a career services advisor who wants to lay the groundwork for the success of your neurodivergent students (whether or not they have disclosed their status), you must ensure that hiring managers are properly prepared to interview and manage neurodivergent interns. Here are some strategies to ensure managers are ready to support a neurodiverse workforce:

- Provide hiring managers with guidance on how to interview all candidates so that neurodivergent candidates are given full consideration. This includes how to provide accommodations to those who disclose that they are neurodivergent.
- Train managers and supervisors on how to effectively work with, supervise, and support neurodivergent employees.
- Make sure each manager understands how to interact in a one-on-one feedback session. These sessions should include regular, appropriate, and effective feedback on what interns or employees

are doing well and constructive feedback on where and how they can improve. (One-on-ones are critical, which is why we will explore them in more depth shortly.)

◆ Ensure that managers are equipped and ready to provide any and all important information through written materials so the intern or employee can easily review and refer to it throughout their internship or employment.

Solution #3: Provide Adequate Support to Students/Employees throughout Their Internships or Onboarding

When a student is engaged in an internship or early in their employment, that's not the time to leave them on their own. Colleges should still be engaged in supporting the intern, and employers need to be ready to fill in any gaps as well.

◆ Support the interns with workshops, taught by experts, whether online or in person. Realize that any training offered must accommodate various learning styles—visual, auditory, or kinesthetic. Tap into your business department (at a university) or HR department (in a workplace), or lean into professional associations, to determine the most critical topics and potential training programs to help. If you can't afford a formal facilitator, you could learn to train on the topics yourself through a train-the-trainer program. Or find free online tools on LinkedIn, YouTube, or consultants' blogs and materials. If you're reading this as a student or employee who is not being offered these learning opportunities, these sources apply to you too!

- Give interns and new hires a chance to practice critical skills one-on-one while receiving feedback from peers and/or an expert. This is a crucial way to reinforce what is taught, so whether it's done on the job or at the university, don't skip it! This can be done in workshops, coaching sessions, or planned sessions to reinforce the learning.
- Give managers this book to read! Or reach out to me for help (which leads to my next point).

Inclusion: Why It Matters to Recruiters and Employers

A 2023 study by Boston Consulting Group (BCG) showed the importance of inclusion, since it ranked as a critical priority for employees. Gabrielle Novacek, a managing director and partner at BCG who helped lead the study stated, "Managers also play a key role in companies . . . We know that inclusion is critical if we want to attract, engage, and retain a diverse workforce. Reporting that they are satisfied with their manager correlated with employees' feelings of inclusion rising by 36 points on our BCG BLISS index, which stands for Bias-Free, Leadership, Inclusion, Safety, and Support, and is a comprehensive, statistically rigorous tool that measures the drivers of inclusion and the value that it delivers."

Solution #4: Lean into Ongoing Coaching to Help Both Interns/ Employees and Managers

You'll hear me preach about coaching more than once, because I think it's critical. A coach is someone who wants you to succeed, and they're trained and experienced in their area. For example, a swimming coach is typically an ex-swimmer who knows how to communicate the absolute best ways to move through the water for speed and safety.

There are several factors that have equipped me as a coach. As someone with a neurodivergent family, I see the symptoms others deal with. And as someone who coaches other neurodivergent adults—and their colleagues and managers—I have learned my topic. Essentially, I have lived in the trenches. Personally, I've had to learn ways to adapt in the workplace. It began during my childhood, when I struggled to read and write, and continued through college, when I struggled to write and make friends. I adapted my own skills by getting tutored in college and finding a major that fit the way my brain worked. Those adaptation skills were then honed by witnessing both good and poor management over the years and eventually working to become the manager of diverse and neurodiverse teams over the decades.

So today, I help neurodivergent employees learn and master the skills to succeed in the workplace. (By the way, many of these skills apply to "life in general" as well!) And I also help managers become more aware of how

to better tap into their employees' unique strengths—
such as by setting SMART goals (covered in Chapter
7) that build confidence and performance. Sometimes
I may recommend accommodations to make these goals
more approachable, but in many cases, I merely suggest
small changes. And you'd be surprised by how simple
yet effective some of these changes are! To illustrate how
outside coaching can help multiple people involved with
a situation, let's explore an example.

An employee, Amanda, was struggling in her interactions with coworkers. While she was pleasant most
of the day, she reportedly spent her first hour at work
"barking" at those around her—not showing her best
side. These reactions made her team want to avoid
her, and the manager was hearing about it. That's why
Amanda got referred to me for coaching.

As we talked, I learned that Amanda's coworkers
arrived around thirty minutes before she did. As soon
as she got to work, someone inevitably would show up
in her office.

"They bombard me with requests—or just conversation—as soon as I walk through the door," she said.
"I never get a chance to settle in."

"How does this make you feel?" I asked.

"Overwhelmed, I guess," she confessed. "I already have a lot of things on my mind to do, and they make me jump off track. It almost feels like I'm getting attacked."

It turned out that what her colleagues perceived as irritable behavior was actually frustration that she couldn't settle into work and organize her own thoughts and tasks. She felt bombarded and unable to focus, so she reacted.

As I thought of solutions for Amanda, I immediately remembered a former boss of mine. He would arrive in the office at 8 a.m., but we learned that he wasn't truly "there" yet. For the first hour, he'd read his email, drink coffee, and prepare for the day. Then, at 9 a.m., he switched on his light as if to say, "Open for business!" We all learned not to engage with him before we saw that light.

"How about if you talk to your coworkers about this and request that if and when they need to discuss something important, they schedule time with you, along with an agenda," I told Amanda. "That way, you'll feel less caught off guard, and you can prepare for the conversations." I knew urgent needs may still come up. But for the majority of these interruptions, I thought this solution would work.

And it did. Amanda implemented this plan, which created some critical boundaries around her time and space. Her colleagues learned to respect these needs, which improved her relationships as well as her ability to stay on task. The manager was happy too!

An outside coach can offer a new perspective for an employee, a manager, or both. This type of coaching can also help assess an intern's unique strengths to ensure they're positioned in a role where they can shine. And a coach can also help a student or employee learn how to maximize their networking, which is our next topic.

Chapter 5

NETWORK IN A NEURODIVERSE WORLD— FIND YOUR FISH IN THE SEA

Depending on your level of introversion or extroversion, you may love or hate networking. Some see it as an exciting chance to make new friends. But many—especially with neurodivergence— would rather muck out elephant stalls than go to a networking meeting.

These meetings may feel like speed dating, and that wouldn't be a bad correlation. At these events, you'll find strangers, possibly feeling a bit desperate, who are thrust together by an event and forced to exchange information quickly in order to assess for a possible match. Are your palms sweating yet? Mine are.

So don't do them. Just skip networking. Let people come to you. After all, if you're worth it, they will find you.

Yes, I'm kidding. You can't skip networking. No one will find you under your rock. So if you can't avoid it, you might as well learn how to do it well while keeping your esteem and emotional health intact. Networking—closely tied to the topic of recruiting—is important for many reasons, whether you're looking for a job or already enmeshed in a company.

Networking in Your Current Role

While this chapter focuses on getting a job, there are benefits of networking even while in your current job:

- You can get to know your colleagues while having fun and helping your career.
- You'll discover what other people in your organization do—gaining awareness of how you may collaborate in the future.
- You'll be reminded of how everybody in the organization has value.
- You may learn new information that increases your job performance.
- You may uncover future openings more quickly.

- You could gain allies and maybe even a mentor.
- You may get feedback from those you meet and get to know.
- You might help someone else!

You'll especially benefit from networking with any stakeholders in a department or role where you're interested in moving, or with people who have a job you find interesting. Start with those you have common ground with, such as within your organization, or with a colleague; this can also help you get an "in" to talk to anyone who is hiring.

My tips for networking are down-and-dirty— meaning I won't limit myself to just one strategy. This is because you'll need to experiment to find what works best for you. But my first tip is the one I find the most critical.

Networking Strategy #1: Get Personal

Your networking should start well before you need a job (or employee, if you're a manager). And it should start outside of any meeting hall or boardroom.

We discussed how to network in your company. But another way to do it is by getting to know your neighbor. Your dog groomer. Your favorite cousin.

And don't just take from them; *give* first. Find out what someone else needs and offer it if you can. Do they need help watering their plants while they're gone? Or setting up their new computer? If you're a job seeker, maybe they even need help with something that taps into the skills you want to amplify in your next role. Did your friend's mom, Georgia, just start an online business selling jewelry? If you're seeking a job as a web designer, consider offering to help set up her site. Not only will you gain experience, but you never know who Georgia knows.

What are you good at, and who can you help? Job referrals are built on the "who you know" philosophy.

If you're looking for work (or to fill a position), once you know someone, you can tell them what type of job you're seeking and see if they know anyone who is hiring. Don't lose heart if they don't have any ideas; it's a numbers game. The more people you know and the more days that go by, the more apt you are to know someone hiring for your next role.

If they say yes, they do know someone, ask for an introduction. But first, make sure you have your resume (or job description, if you're the one hiring) up-to-date and fully edited.

There are many online tools for resume writing, but I recommend you also reach out to an editor or job coach to help. Minimally, ask a literate friend or family member to review your materials before you send them.

Networking with a Serial Networker

My editor told me about getting her first "real" job after college. Jocelyn is an introvert who sometimes experiences social anxiety, and she didn't enjoy networking. After graduating and returning to her small town, she was struggling to land a job in her field. (This was before the Internet!) Then one day, her mom called her, excited.

"I went in to have a VHS home video copied, and the place that did it is *amazing*! And they want to interview you!" her mom said.

Unsure what this "place" did, Jocelyn carried her resume into the office and met with the owner. Two hours later—after helping to edit a TV commercial—she was offered a job. (Turns out, it was an ad agency.) This launched her career in communications and eventually led to her owning a business.

Jocelyn didn't like networking, but her mom was a serial networker—someone who never met a stranger and wasn't afraid to "talk up" anyone she thought highly of. If you aren't fluent at networking, who do you know who is? Think of someone who is friendly and seems to know everyone. (This might be someone with the strength of *connectedness* as discussed in Chapter 2.) Can you get to know them better and let them know you're looking for a job?

Networking Strategy #2: Get Out There

Yes, attend networking events. If you aren't sure where to start, try joining associations in your industry. Rather than list them here, I recommend you do a web search for "professional associations" along with your industry or role, and you'll find hundreds to choose from. Look at their websites and search their calendar of events. They often hold monthly meetings and annual or semi-annual conferences. These are great places to meet people (refer to strategy #1!) or even attend sessions to boost your knowledge and skills. Many will even offer workshops on topics outside of their industry niche. For example, Project Management Institute doesn't focus only on Scrum or Agile; they also teach leadership and change management skills. And if you're in a profession where you need continuing education (CE) credits, these conferences can also help you stay up-to-date with requirements.

Speaking

As the joke goes (perhaps first told by Jerry Seinfeld), at a funeral, many would rather be the one in the casket than the person delivering the eulogy. This is because public speaking is regularly cited as people's greatest fear, often ranked above death itself! But if you're someone who enjoys the spotlight, consider trying to speak at an association event. This could allow you to showcase your knowledge, practice your speaking skills, and meet people. Associations are attended by professionals from numerous companies, so if a leader hears you speak, they may approach you afterward for more information or to utilize your skills.

How do you break in to speak at these groups? Associations are typically looking for speakers at their monthly meetings and conferences. Reach out to their meeting planners to inquire, and you may need to submit a proposal (often called a "call for proposal" or "request for proposal") or topic description with learning objectives (which allows them to get it approved for credits) along with your bio. If you need help with writing these, ask someone versed in marketing and editing.

Some of the greatest public speakers are neurodivergent. Keynote speaker Sam Glenn, who motivates thousands every year with his on-stage paintings, humor, and inspiration, leans into his ADD. "I have fun with it," he states, "And the audience does too! I consider it my super-power because it allows me to create speeches that don't bore people. Instead, audiences learn because my humor is sticky, and they leave refreshed and supercharged."

Networking Strategy #3: Get Online

For many, this is the easiest way to network because it allows someone to "hide" behind a computer screen. This comes with advantages and drawbacks. While it allows you to network from the comfort of your living room, it's also easy to get lost in the sea of job-seekers.

You may end up feeling like you're bobbing around in a dingy within a massive ocean.

But don't give up on establishing your presence online. LinkedIn can be a great place to research companies, connect with hiring managers or department heads, and find job postings. They even have settings that allow you to display to your network that you're looking for work.

Again, whenever possible, it's best to make personal connections. This doesn't mean you must meet someone in-person, but you do need to think about how you might offer value to others. Just reaching out to a stranger and saying, "I need a job. Are you hiring?" isn't usually the best approach. Instead, consider sharing valuable content online that might help a manager in your industry. You may blog or create short articles if writing is your strength. Or create videos or a podcast to share if you're creative, inspiring, or have informative tips to offer.

You can use other social media too, such as Facebook, Instagram, YouTube, Threads, and Snapchat. Realize some of these are more professional than others, but depending on your desired role, they may be appropriate.

What Happens Online Stays Online

Las Vegas isn't the only place where embarrassing things happen that you'd rather forget or "delete." With ready access to your phone and the "share" button, it's easy to post something you'll later regret. Many hiring managers and university admissions counselors will search a candidate's online presence to get a feel for who they are. Avoid presenting yourself with red flags—like drunken photos, extreme political or religious rants, or overly negative or revealing statements. Even if your profiles are marked as private, someone in your network could see these and not want to recommend you to a hiring manager they know. And with AI becoming savvier at finding information, privacy becomes harder to enforce. What you "put out there" becomes part of your personal brand. And while it's fine and advisable to be personable and relatable, you must always consider the impression you're giving to someone who doesn't know (and love) you as well as your mom does.

This applies if you're a hiring manager as well. Candidates could be looking at you! And if you represent a company, advocate for ensuring your corporate social media and web presence are kept professional and up-to-date. To that end, make it a practice to quickly answer any customer inquiries or complaints you receive!

Networking (and Interviewing) Strategy #4: Get Practicing

Many who are neurodivergent struggle with making small talk. My solution is this: Practice!

Who do you start with? My friend recently told me a story that illustrates a clever idea. Jaime was feeling insecure and introverted at a dinner after he'd spoken for the group. So he found someone who looked as miserable as he felt.

"Fellow introvert?" Jaime asked the woman.

"Yes," she admitted.

"Good. If we stand next to each other, we'll both look 'normal.'"

They shared a laugh at Jaime's joke and did just that. Before long, they started talking to each other. Then a few other people came and joined them. By starting with one person and warming up, Jaime felt more comfortable talking to others. This story illustrates two points.

First: *Talking to others gets easier with practice.* And second: *Most likely, someone else in the room is as nervous or uncomfortable as you are.*

When talking to someone new, realize that you'll be expected to share information about yourself, but you can always turn around and ask questions of the other person. Not only does this take the heat off of you temporarily, but it also allows the other person to share—which often leads to a feeling of connection and empathy.

When networking, memorize some standard questions you can ask and practice them with a friend, family member, or coach. Roleplay different scenarios. Personal questions may include:

- "Where do you work?"
- "What do you enjoy most about your job?"
- "What challenges are you currently facing at work?"
- "What hobbies do you enjoy?"
- "Do you do much traveling? If so, what are some of your favorite locations?
- "Have you read any good books recently or watched any good movies or TV shows? Can you recommend any?"

If you're interviewing for a job, research the company first, and come prepared with a list of questions. They may include:

- "What does a typical day in my role look like?"
- "What skills and traits are you looking for?"
- "Can you tell me a bit more about [insert a company program or detail you found online or through a contact]?"
- "How would you describe your workplace culture?"

Don't interrogate the other person in this process; leave time for them to answer fully. Listen for cues to follow up with additional questions so you can learn more. Then chime in with your own ideas when appropriate. For example, if they like a TV show that you also enjoy, you can state something like, "I love *The Office* too! I especially love the character, Michael, and the time he almost drove his car into a lake. Who's your favorite character?"

If you're a recruiter, you may be seasoned at asking and answering questions. But since you're human, you may also get nervous—or you may not know how to ask good questions that highlight a person's strengths, especially when they're neurodivergent. Realize that the other person may struggle to answer, but that doesn't mean they aren't intelligent and capable. Give them a chance to highlight their strengths. Again: Treat them like an individual!

Now that you're versed in recruiting and networking, it's time to focus on what to do when in the role. Onboarding is one of my favorite topics for managers and employees, so let's dive in!

Chapter 6

ONBOARD NEURODIVERSE EMPLOYEES—THE FIRST WORK WEEK

If networking is like speed dating, then onboarding is like the honeymoon period when everything is new, sparkly, and exciting.

Or at least it should be. The truth is, onboarding isn't as easy as falling in love. It requires a specific process to ensure it's done right, especially for neurodivergent employees. And since it's not typically a matchmaking between only two people—but more like the blending of different fish pods—you must consider many components.

In this chapter, we'll explore how to get the most out of your onboarding process. Whether you're a manager or employee, this will ensure that your initial "love match" lasts and grows. Instead of allowing bad habits to fester or misinformation to spread, the right onboarding clarifies expectations while welcoming the employee into their new "school."

Clarifying Expectations from the First Day

You only get one chance to make a first impression. Onboarding is your company's and your team's opportunity to do that. For me as a manager, that involves helping my new employee feel like they made the right decision. While it's exciting to land a job, the idea of actually going to work can feel scary—especially if someone struggles with social interactions, interpreting nuanced language, being overstimulated, following directions, and the myriad of other challenges facing the neurodivergent.

As a manager, unless an employee discloses that they're neurodivergent, you may suspect but won't know. The best way to get off on the right foot in this case is by clarifying expectations early—even before someone walks through the door for their first day. Being clear up front will go a long way in easing tensions that may inhibit learning and productivity.

Many companies have their HR department send out an email after an employee accepts an offer. This includes a list of items that must be completed prior to the employee's first day at work. It's a little impersonal and, to a first-time and neurodiverse employee, can be a little intimidating. It may look a little like this:

Hello Grant,

Welcome. We are delighted that you are joining ABC Company, and we are looking forward to the contributions we will make together.

Now that pre-employment screens are completed, we are pleased to confirm your start date of 01/01/2027, reporting to Sally Smith.

Listed below are the next steps in this process, which we ask you to complete in a timely manner:

- The Form I-9 Section 1 (Employee Eligibility Verification) request has been sent to your personal email address. Once you receive the email, don't delay in completing Section 1 prior to your start date. The email will appear as follows:
  - From Email Address: noreply@company.com
  - Subject Line: Company Employment Eligibility (I-9) Form

- The Onboarding Activation email has been sent to your personal email address requesting you to log in to kickstart your onboarding forms and process. This is a one-time initial login. Please ensure you complete your onboarding forms as soon as possible in order to avoid delays within the process. The email will appear as follows:

- □   From Email Address: recruiting@company.com
- □   Subject Line: Welcome to Company Onboarding— Action Required!

Details on your arrival/start time and other important items for your first day will be provided by your manager. If you have not heard from your manager, please contact them directly at the email address provided to you during the recruitment process.

You will receive additional correspondence from Information Technology on how to log in to your computer on your first day, as well as other helpful resources to prepare you to thrive. We look forward to seeing you soon.

Sincerely,

HR

This letter includes items that **HR** needs for onboarding. As a manager, however, I never like to leave everything up to **HR**. I love to be the supervisor who follows up with a personal email. For that reason, I have my own personal onboarding checklist, which I'm including here. Your list may include different action points, but these are some helpful topics to cover.

**PREPARING FOR YOUR EMPLOYEE'S FIRST WORK WEEK—
A MANAGER'S CHECKLIST**

1. Send an email welcoming them to the company and team. Include:
   - Their start date and time
   - A reminder to complete all forms
   - A list of who they will meet with when they come in
   - The dress code
   - Whether you will be taking them to lunch
   - The time you will be meeting with them for your first one-on-one
2. Contact IT to ensure the employee will have access to their phone, computer, etc.
3. Make sure they have access to a desk or workspace on their first day.
4. Ensure that their ID badge will be ready.
5. Work with HR to obtain their onboarding schedule.
6. Determine and/or obtain their training schedule.
7. Identify a peer mentor who can help them.
8. Identify a community mentor to support them.

The following is a sample email I send to new onsite employees. For a remote employee, I schedule a Zoom call for onboarding (and follow-up one-on-one meetings).

Good morning, Grant:

I am so excited to have you join our team. Your start date will be 01/01/2027. I will meet you at the front door marked Main Entrance at 9:00 a.m. (Please do not use the entrance for surgeons that you will see as you first enter the driveway.)

We offer a casual work environment. Most employees wear jeans or khakis to the office. I believe you saw that when you came in for the interview.

I will be able to take you to the cafeteria for coffee and then walk you to your desk from 9:00 to 10:00 a.m. At that time, I will drop you off with your peer mentor, Jonathan Smith. Jonathan will introduce you to the rest of the team and take you to lunch.

You are then scheduled to begin orientation with HR at 1:00 p.m. in conference room 101. Jonathan will drop you off there after lunch. Orientation will end each day at 5:00 p.m., and HR will hand you your security badge at the end of class on the first day. Orientation will conclude on Thursday afternoon.

I have scheduled our first one-on-one for 9:15 a.m. on Friday of your first week. We can meet in the cafeteria for coffee.

I am looking forward to seeing you again and having you as a member of our team.

Sincerely,

Lee

If you're the new employee, you'll also want to make the right impression for that first day. Following is my checklist to help ensure that your first day and week go smoothly. (If you're in Career Services, feel free to offer this or a similar list to your students.)

**PREPARING FOR YOUR FIRST WORK WEEK—
AN EMPLOYEE'S CHECKLIST**

BEFORE YOU ARRIVE:

1. Complete all HR paperwork on time
2. Complete drug test if required
3. Send your manager an email confirming:
   - Time
   - Entrance
   - Dress code
   - Expectations and/or plans for the day
   - Map out route to work

ON YOUR FIRST DAY:

1. Get your security/ID badge, if applicable.
2. If in-person, learn your way around the building, including your workspace.
   - Find the bathrooms.
   - Find the cafeteria or lunchroom.
3. Schedule time to meet with your boss. (See "Template for First One-on-One with Supervisor.")
4. Confirm the date(s) for any onboarding classes.
5. Start to set up times to meet with coworkers if possible or meet with them informally.
   - Listen to what they do.
   - Ask what they like and what they struggle with.

ONCE YOU GET YOUR PC (TYPICALLY DURING YOUR FIRST WEEK):

1. Learn how to use the company's intranet (if they have one).

    - This is the internal network where you can explore policies for HR (including employee assistance programs), finance, and travel.

    - You may also be able to view the company's org chart, employee directory, scheduling and/or project management tools, strategic goals, and more.

    - Especially if working remotely, learn the platform that your meetings will be held on (such as Zoom, Google Meet, or Microsoft Teams).

2. Learn how and when to complete timesheets and expense reports (if applicable).

3. Read any available standard operating procedures (SOPs).

4. Start any online training required, such as for systems access and compliance, cybersecurity, safety, and so on.

5. Learn who your internal and external customers are. This is your first chance to network and gain some allies. If applicable or appropriate, meet some customers, using this time to *listen* and *learn*.

Show Empathy and Engage Your Employees

The ideal time to think about retaining your best employees is on the first day, and it starts by engaging them. *Employee engagement* is the discretionary effort an employee decides to invest into their role. Every company has a minimum standard of performance each employee must meet to keep their job. An engaged employee goes several steps beyond to deliver more than is required—because they want to. We discovered the downsides of disengagement in Chapter 1. If a lack of engagement costs US companies trillions of dollars per year, how can we ensure that we have it?

Employee engagement boils down to this: Treat people like humans. Whether you're an employee or manager, you deserve to be treated well. Research shows time and again that people don't leave jobs; they leave their supervisors. And they're leaving because they don't feel valued and appreciated.

Essentially, they crave empathy. And if they don't get it, they are prone to looking elsewhere. Some version of empathy is also tied into nearly every organizational mission statement. And empathy helps to foster the *psychological safety* team members need to perform well—a concept reinforced by a large study, Project Aristotle, conducted at Google.

So what is *empathy*? At its core, empathy involves anticipating what someone else needs by sitting in their seat and doing your best to understand their perspective. You've probably heard of the Golden Rule: *Do unto others as you would have them do unto you.* I'd like to raise the ante and recommend the Platinum Rule: *Do unto others as they want done unto them.* As we've discussed, not everyone has the same strengths and needs. You can't expect to engage everyone in the same ways.

Missed Promotion

Sometimes people with neurodivergence are perceived as lacking empathy, even if that's not the case.

My husband, Scott, was the head of his class and able to do math in his head like a whiz kid. So later when the time came for him to be considered for a work promotion, he thought he had it in the bag. Assuming the advancement would be based on the quality of his work, he believed he was a shoe-in.

But the support staff saw him differently. They viewed him as abrasive when they made mistakes, wearing his frustration like a crazy hat that you can't miss. He failed to use the appropriate filter due to his neurodivergence and lack of leadership skills. These same support staff were close to the CEO. When they reported on his attitude, it cost him the promotion. Scott paid the price for what appeared to be his lack of empathy. It's not that he didn't care, but at the time, he didn't know how to show his staff that he did.

Today, Scott is the vice president of a department and is known for his style of one-on-ones and providing timely feedback. He is also known for caring about his team's family lives and asking about their career goals. But those are traits he had to learn how to show, partly due to his neurodivergence.

How you show up is important. If you want to be a leader or to be noticed positively by your leaders, treat everyone with respect and empathy. If this is something you struggle with, don't be afraid to seek out a coach or mentor to help you.

Empathy involves showing that you care about a neurodivergent person's unique challenges, even as you recognize their strengths. Empathy also requires that you listen effectively (a topic covered more in Chapter 8 on communication).

It all boils down to this. As a manager, how would you want your grandmother to be treated if she were sick in the hospital? Do that. How would you want your baby sister to be managed if she dreamed of reaching the C-suite? Mentor your employee that way. What if your neighbor had lost a child? Show that compassion. Consider the scenarios that happen to any human, and realize whether you know it or not, these events are happening in the lives of your employees. Added to that, your neurodivergent employees are likely facing challenges with *just fitting in* and doing their day-to-day tasks that you may not see or consider. This is important to consider during onboarding.

Equity Versus Equality

You've probably heard about people needing to be treated *equally*. However, *equality* and *equity* are not the same thing. Equality means everyone gets the same treatment no matter what, which isn't realistic or advised. Equity means treatment is tailored to each individual—based on their strengths, limitations, and preferences—in a way that allows each person the same opportunity to flourish. Even with formal DEI programs vanishing in many companies, with a neurodiverse workforce (and many other hidden and overt disabilities), managers must find ways to provide equity if they wish to attract and retain their best talent.

Accommodations—How Do I Navigate?

The topic of accommodations at work can often seem befuddling for two reasons.

First, many employees wrestle with whether to divulge a disability up front. Doing so could lead to better accommodations; and for some, this is crucial. But for those with less limiting or obvious disabilities, including some neurodivergent employees, they can choose whether to disclose their condition.

By law, the American Disabilities Act (ADA) protects those with disabilities, which it defines as someone who:

- Has a physical or mental impairment that substantially limits one or more major life activities,
- Has a history or record of such an impairment (such as cancer that is in remission), or
- Is perceived by others as having such an impairment (such as a person who has scars from a severe burn).

As the ADA states, "Because the ADA is a law, and not a benefit program, you do not need to apply for coverage."

But there is some discrepancy over what qualifies as a disability. Someone with neurodivergence may qualify under the "mental impairment" clause. But this isn't always clearcut, and some who are neurodivergent prefer not to disclose their diagnoses. One reason for this is that unfortunately, revealing a disability risks potential backlash through discrimination or unconscious bias. One participant in a recent survey I conducted stated, "At a recent job, I disclosed that I dealt with several issues regarding being neurodivergent. I asked for a medical leave of absence and was fired while on medical leave." While I'm not privy to her employer's reasons for letting her go, these consequences do happen regardless of our laws.

To Disclose a Disability or Not

The decision to disclose a health or mental condition is personal. I can't share absolutes on this, but I'll offer some guidelines.

If you were hired into a company that offers a targeted neurodiversity hiring and/or employment program, divulging your neurodivergence may allow you to shine and receive much-needed assistance. If they value neurodiversity enough to hire for it, chances are greater (but not zero) that you'll avoid discrimination when disclosing it.

If your company isn't open with their policy, consider the severity of your limitations and needs. Does your workplace already offer sufficient accommodations? Or could they, if you asked? Even without formally disclosing your condition, you may be able to advocate for what you need. If the lighting isn't automatically set, for example, consider saying, "I'm light sensitive; do you mind if I dim the lights slightly while we meet?" Or work with noise cancellation earphones if you're easily distracted. These simple modifications don't reveal neurodivergence since many neurotypical people are also light or sound sensitive.

The second reason why the topic of accommodations can get muddled is because employers are often worried about getting it wrong—either by overlooking a disability need or by appearing as though they're favoring one employee by offering something "special."

Again, the concept of equity versus equality works here; the goal of accommodations isn't to make everyone equal in all ways, but rather to give everyone an equitable opportunity to succeed. For many disabilities, the need for accommodations is obvious. A diabetic needs access to insulin and glucose, for example. Someone using a wheelchair needs readily accessible ramps and restrooms. Providing these doesn't give those individuals any leg up over their abled coworkers. It functions similarly for the neurodivergent; just because you can't see their limitations or quantify their threats, those conditions may be hindering those employees from doing their best work.

Here's a simple example to illustrate the concept of equity. Imagine two people tasked with keeping stats for a lacrosse game. Except instead of sitting on the sidelines, they're watching from over a tall, wooden fence. The taller person can see the game by just standing and looking. But the shorter person sees nothing. If you give the shorter person a stool to stand on, they suddenly would have an equitable (but not equal) opportunity to see the game.

Now imagine there's a third person in a wheelchair. This person can't see by standing on the stool. They need a platform upon which to watch.

In this scenario, all three are equally capable of recording the plays; in fact, maybe the person in the wheelchair is the *best* at math and documentation. By offering this accommodation, you're providing equitable opportunities for each so that they can shine based on the skills they were hired for. And you're getting the results your company needs.

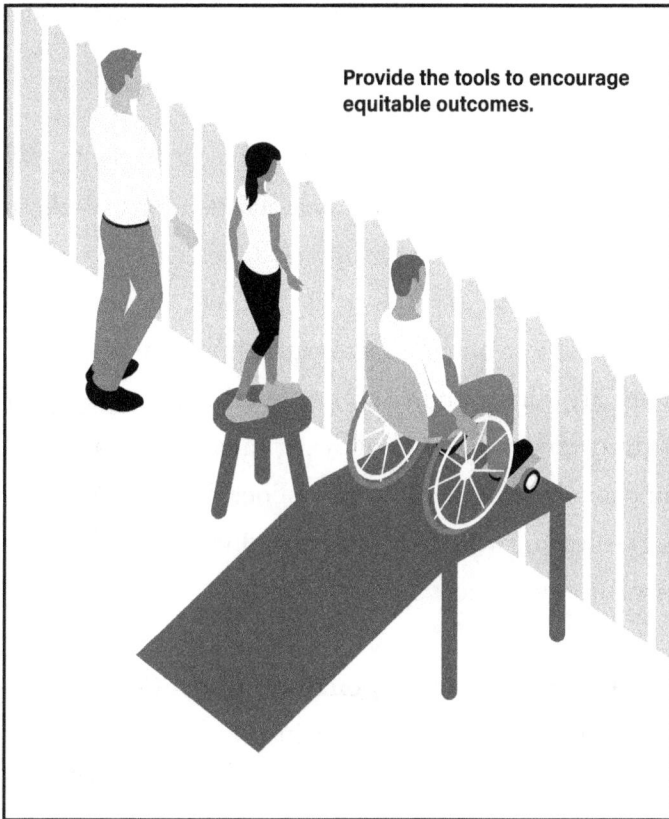

Provide the tools to encourage equitable outcomes.

As a manager, aim to provide "stools to stand on," "ramps," and "platforms"—in a literal or metaphorical sense, based on the employees' needs—so they may do their jobs more efficiently and effectively without a lot of fanfare around requesting accommodations. A survey I conducted found that 60 percent of neurodivergent employees don't know what accommodations they're entitled to, and nearly half aren't sure who they would go to for assistance.

Another recent survey showed that 72.1 percent of neurodivergent people are very likely, or likely, to stay if their organization offers accommodations. Without accommodations, that drops to 31.6 percent. If you care about retention, this statistic should get your attention.

Whether you offer formal accommodations or not, there are some simple ways to proactively equip your neurodiverse workforce, allowing them to tap into what functions best for them. These options should be available regardless of whether someone divulges a disability or neurodivergence:

- **If you have an open floor plan, offer alternative spaces.** This may include work-from-home options, an office with a door (if accepted for this person's position), or a quiet place to take a break.
- **Offer more subdued lighting.** Consider dimming lights (while also being sensitive to anyone with vision impairment).
- **Be mindful of loud noises, such as music.** Music may be a great ice breaker, but for someone who is sound sensitive, this can be unbearable. Ensure that your volume levels are reasonable

and check in to ensure people are comfortable. A simple, "How is the volume?" allows someone who is over-stimulated to speak up without standing out.

* **Encourage earplugs, noise-cancellation earphones, or "migraine" eyeglasses.** These tools can help reduce stimulation, so make them fully acceptable in your culture. While you can't likely buy all these tools, earplugs are inexpensive and discreet.

* **Allow people to move around when needed.** Take breaks during meetings or offer movement as part of your learning activities.

* **Encourage items for "stimming."** This includes small squishable toys or other sensory items that can occupy someone's hands (and extra energy) during meetings or focused work. These can be especially helpful for those with ADD. You can bring a basket of them to meetings, make them available on your desk for use during one-on-ones, or simply normalize them if someone wants to bring their own. Choose items that don't make noise, since one person's solution might aggravate their office mate!

If you're an employee who isn't being offered these accommodations but needs them, ask your supervisor. Assume they want you to succeed! Here are some simple steps to follow when bringing this up with your manager:

1. Briefly state the problem (with supporting data).
2. Explain the impact of the problem (translating to productivity).
3. Offer one or more solutions (with documentation as to why they are effective solutions) and their cost.
4. Summarize your proposed solution and ask for verification or approval.

As you do this, make sure that the costs are realistic and that the impacts are not overstated.

Addressing Accommodations Holistically

What's helpful to one employee might be distracting to another. That's why it's important to consider accommodations in the context of the whole team, whether you're a manager or employee.

I once had an employee, Isaac, who clicked his pen all day to self-soothe, which I learned was thoroughly annoying and distracting the rest of the team. The solution was simple: I found a stress ball and a rubber band for him to fiddle with (quietly). I spoke to Isaac privately about the pen clicking, and he began using the quieter items. This made him and the team happy.

Onboarding into Your Culture

Not all companies include cultural onboarding, but the ones who do are doing it right. Your culture training might include interactions, videos, or materials that share:

- Organizational mission, values, and strategic vision, and what they mean
- Stories of internal and external customers and their successes—such as employee accomplishments and thrilled customer testimonials
- Traits that make your company unique and enjoyable—such as awards, special events throughout the year, lunch-and-learn programs, and social opportunities

Consider this process like meeting a new cousin you didn't know you had. When you invite Alison to come visit your family, even if she's looked over your social media profiles, she would likely still be curious about who you really are. To "onboard" Alison into your family, you might tell her about your son Kyle's division-one college basketball scholarship (sharing success stories). You may detail service projects your family is a part of (hinting at your mission and values). You may take Alison to your daughter Ruth's preschool play (sharing activities). Think of your hired employee like a new family member visiting for the first time. Besides telling them "the bathroom is down the hall," share the intangibles that make your workplace delightful.

In effect, this is about creating shared stories and experiences amongst employees that help to define what your workplace "pod of fish" is all about.

Consider assigning a cultural ambassador who can champion the great things about your workplace, and schedule your employee to have lunch with them. In such informal sessions, the onboarding employee can ask questions and maybe hear fun stories that only come out in personal interactions—akin to hearing about the time young Sally accidentally put salt instead of sugar into the cookies she took to her second-grade class, leading to a big surprise at snack time.

Onboarding is just as much about preparing new employees to understand the organization's building layout, policies, and procedures as it is about meeting coworkers, building a relationship with an immediate supervisor, understanding one's role, and learning about the company's culture. Many organizations excel in some of their onboarding practices, but few conduct a comprehensive onboarding experience for neurotypical employees, much less neurodiverse employees. Since engagement is linked to both employee performance and retention, the best onboarding practices create processes to integrate new hires as quickly and effectively as possible, so they can start adding value to the team and organization.

Chapter 7

ONE-ON-ONES—
A MANAGER'S AND
EMPLOYEE'S MOST
CRITICAL TOOL

As a manager or employee, your one-on-one meetings are critical for sharing information, setting expectations, and improving performance. These sessions are paramount as they set the stage for your communications and coaching endeavors. In this chapter, we'll explore the framework for how they're done.

A Manager's Role in the First One-on-One

As a manager, one of the most important meetings you'll have with your new employee as part of the onboarding process is the first one-on-one. This is your opportunity to help them relax into their new "pod of fish" while also establishing the ground rules.

It's critical to schedule your first one-on-one early—within their first week, if not on the first day. It may be appropriate to do this meeting in two steps. Your objectives as you meet include:

1. Getting to know them and letting them get to know you
2. Clarifying your expectations around communications and performance

If you're a manager meeting with an employee in their first one-on-one, consider not only how they'll serve your company, but how your company will make them feel welcome. Not only will this make your work environment more pleasant, but it will also save you time, effort, and money in having to rehire when someone leaves due to feeling like a fish out of water.

Objective #1: Get to Know Your Employee— What Matters?

As a manager working to onboard a new employee, get to know what makes them tick. Over time, you'll discover more details about their lives and personality.

This will help you know how to relate to and engage them. Up front, here are some traits and preferences you can uncover:

- **Strengths.** We discussed strengths in Chapter 3, and onboarding is when the rubber meets the road. Discover what makes your employee shine! (Hopefully you learned some strengths in their recruiting process too.)

- **Introversion Versus Extroversion.** An introvert may not want to be rewarded with a company dinner, preferring a gift certificate to enjoy a nice meal at home with a loved one (or their pet ferret), whereas an extrovert may thrive with public recognition at an awards banquet.

- **Physical Ability.** Asking people to "stand up" as an ice breaker when some team members are in a wheelchair or in chronic pain may not be received well, whereas someone who runs marathons may love a walk-and-talk to break up the monotony of a meeting.

- **Cultural and Life Background.** Your employees likely don't all share the same religion, family stories, or values. Be sensitive and inclusive, showing genuine interest when someone tries to share about their mores or preferences. Your seasonal salutation of "Merry Christmas" lands better when said by a priest in a Catholic church than it would in a multicultural all-employee meeting.

• **Neurodiversity.** Someone with ASD may not want to engage in conversation about their home-life, whereas someone else might light up—and talk more than you expected (or wanted!)—over a topic they're enthusiastic about, like the picture on their desk of them fishing with a grandparent. Be sensitive when asking questions, showing curiosity but backing off if you sense resistance. (And learn the questions you must never ask unless you want HR knocking on your door!)

• **Learning Styles.** Some people learn best by reading or viewing diagrams (*visual learners*). Others prefer to hear lectures (*auditory learners*). Still, others want to see a concept demonstrated and then try it themselves (*kinesthetic learners*). It's helpful to know your own learning style and to learn the styles of those around you. Not only will this help others ask for information in the way they can best retain it, but you can also then tailor your communications. (Learning styles tie heavily into various neurodivergent diagnoses.)

Objective #2: Clarify Your Expectations

You'll have a much easier time managing an employee's performance if they know up front what you expect. It's especially important to clarify your expectations around:

- **Communications.** This includes sharing your (and their) preferred communication style and frequency. Do you plan to hold weekly one-on-one meetings to get updates on project progress? Do you prefer biweekly emails summarizing what's been done and any outstanding questions? Clarify up front what you expect and ask for feedback on what works best for them. Explain that your goal is to help them shine!
- **Performance: Setting SMART Goals.** What do you want your employee to *do*? I can't stress enough that unless you've been crystal clear about what you expect in regard to your employee's work goals, you can't expect them to get it right. Stating what you expect builds a sense of confidence and competence that we all crave as

individuals. This is how your employee can shine and even get promoted down the road. Then ask them to repeat back to you their understanding of the expectation.

More on SMART Goals

The need for clear expectations is why I'm adamant about setting SMART goals or tasks. SMART goals aren't new or groundbreaking, but this type of goal-setting is absolutely crucial with the neurodivergent because they need concrete direction. Saying, "I want you to write a report about what your team has been doing," is very different than saying, "I want you to write an 800 to 1,000-word summary of the progress in our new budgeting initiative over the past month, and deliver it to me via email by next Friday, January 24. This will help us in our meeting the following Wednesday, January 29, as we plan the next month's tasks." Notice how this qualifies as a SMART task:

- **Specific**: It states exactly what you want—a written update on the project.
- **Measurable**: It should be 800 to 1,000 words.

* **Achievable**: This isn't too big of a task for one week.
* **Relevant**: It will help you plan the team's work over the next month.
* **Time-Bound**: It's due next Friday.

The most important concept here is that goals should not be wishy-washy and abstract. Instead, they should be crystal clear so that you'll know once they're met. Especially when dealing with neurodivergence like ASD, it's crucial to be transparent in your expectations. And if you're neurodivergent, you know how a solid plan of action helps you avoid the guessing game over what to do next.

Using the following chart, try mapping out a current SMART goal that you need to assign an employee or do yourself. State the goal in the top row and then define how it meets each component of SMART.

YOUR GOAL	
SPECIFIC	
MEASURABLE	
ACHIEVABLE	
RELEVANT	
TIME-BOUND	

It takes effort to make your tasks and goals SMART, but this will save you time later. If everyone is clear about what needs to get done, when, and why, you won't be backpedaling to correct miscommunications or missed goals later.

SMART goals aren't rigid; they can be adapted as you learn more, applying an agile mindset. But even those changes should be made intentionally, in a way that's measured and meaningful. They can also be tracked during the one-on-one process, so there are no surprises as the year progresses. Goals can also be changed as the company's priorities shift during the year.

Managers: Ten Best Practices for Conducting One-on-Ones

As you engage in these meetings or coaching sessions, realize that some cues a neurotypical person may pick up on may not be as easily assimilated by someone neurodivergent. Those with ASD, for example, may struggle to read body language or interpret sarcasm (as we discussed in Chapter 2). Following are ten best practices to help these meetings become more productive. Many of these tips apply to coaching in general as well.

Best Practice #1: Be Patient and Flexible

Offer multiple ways for others to learn so you can establish a relationship and foster performance.

A Literally Confusing Instruction

As a manager, I once told an employee after our one-on-one, "I'd like you to check in with me regularly for updates on how it's going with our biggest customer." Okay, that seems clear enough, right? Except to this neurodivergent employee, it wasn't.

"Hello Lee, I'm here for an update," he said from my office door an hour later. Of course I had no updates. I had meant for him to show up in around a week, not that day! What I failed to do is make the task SMART.

While your expectations may seem obvious to you, your employees are not mind-readers. And someone who is neurodivergent may especially struggle with directions that aren't ultra clear.

Best Practice #2: Avoid Jargon

Using acronyms, unfamiliar industry-speak, or company slang is likely to confuse new employees. If you must use these words, translate them early on. Once, before I was going to be interviewed for a position, a friend who worked in the same company sent me a dictionary of the company's jargon. This allowed me to speak to my interviewers and understand them during the process. It gave me an advantage during the interview.

Best Practice #3: Speak as Clearly as Possible

Especially as you learn your employee's style and strengths, speaking clearly is critical. Some neurodivergent employees will take you very literally, as I shared earlier in this chapter. If you say, "I will be back in five minutes," they will wait exactly five minutes.

Best Practice #4: Break Your Agenda—and an Employee's Tasks—into Smaller Items

Neurodivergent people often struggle with focus, or their mind may work differently in terms of organizing and synthesizing directions. Grouping content can provide clarity while keeping them engaged in what you're saying. And breaking down tasks into subtasks is very helpful.

Best Practice #5: Try Other Ways of Getting Your Point Across

I am a visual learner. While explaining to my team what I wanted, if I wasn't getting my point across, I would often draw a picture. If you're struggling to impart your intended meaning, ask yourself: *Can I encapsulate this point in a clear chart or image? Can I orient the headings or rows to illustrate my meaning?* If you're struggling to understand someone else, consider asking: "Can you show me these comparisons in a visual format?" With a drawing or chart, we can often discuss, analyze, and collaborate on a better idea. Sometimes a picture truly is worth a thousand words!

Best Practice #6: Allow Time to Ask and Answer Questions

Your one-on-ones—including your first—should not be lectures. To avoid this, be proactive and ask questions. If you're the manager, ask, "Do you have any questions for me about what we've gone over or about our organization or your job?"

Best Practice #7: Use Active Listening

Listening can help you de-escalate or avoid confrontation, and it also allows you to learn so you can brainstorm better solutions. We all feel better when we know we've been heard, and this applies to your employees too. (See more on this in the next chapter on communications.)

Best Practice #8: Ask Employees to Repeat Back What They Heard from You

This ensures mutual understanding of expectations. Then listen and respond thoroughly. Leave yourself adequate time to address any questions.

Best Practice #9: Take Notes

If both parties take notes, you're more apt to capture anything critical.

Best Practice #10: Set Your Next One-on-One

As a manager, get used to giving feedback regularly and making yourself available. Let your new hire know when they can expect to see you again in a formal setting. I typically recommend that the second one-on-one be run by the employee, not the manager, so that the employee can get questions answered and take ownership of their progress.

Employees thrive with feedback along the way on how well they're assimilating. Your goal is to make it so there are no surprises in their annual performance review because you've communicated clearly all year long and addressed any concerns or behavior issues as they arise.

An Employee's Role in the One-on-One—Strategies to Make Them Productive

If you're an employee, your one-on-ones are also critical for you. This is a chance for you to do the following:

- Highlight your accomplishments.
- Highlight any continued project hurdles. (But don't spend too much time here; use team meetings instead for this.)
- Align with your manager on priorities.

- Provide feedback for your manager about your needs.
- Receive feedback from your manager about what they need and how you're doing.
- Discuss your career goals.
- Learn about other positions in the organization.

The following eight strategies can help you as you go into your one-on-ones.

Strategy #1: Be Respectful, but Make Yourself a Priority

Your one-on-ones are designed to equip you, so it's up to you to ensure they're helping. If you aren't clear about something, this is your chance to get answers.

Strategy #2: Come Prepared with Questions

Having pre-planned questions will put you at ease if you get nervous, and it will ensure you don't miss anything. You can always ask more questions as they arise.

Strategy #3: Take Notes When Your Supervisor Speaks

Document answers to your questions and feedback on how you're doing or what your supervisor needs from you. Besides helping you remember this information later, note-taking is an accommodation if you struggle with focus or eye contact.

Strategy #4: Repeat Back What You Heard

Make sure that you understand the same instructions as your boss. This way, you'll both be confident in the next steps.

Strategy #5: Lean into Your Learning Style

If you're a visual learner, consider drawing a picture of what you believe the finished project will look like. You can even consider asking this of your manager, if you feel it would help you understand and perform better.

Strategy #6: Let Your Manager Know What You Need

If something isn't working for you or if you need more specific direction from them, this is your chance to ask. An effective manager wants to know where you have obstacles, so they can help you remove them. And they want to know what has worked well, so they can repeat those strategies.

Strategy #7: Send Your Meeting Notes to Your Supervisor Later

Documenting and sending the meeting minutes for confirmation that everything was captured correctly is one more way to avoid miscommunication. I've learned if something isn't documented, it's like it never happened! Especially if HR needs to get involved later, you'll need this documentation. (HR doesn't exist to be "your friend." They are there to do their job and ensure that laws and policies are followed at work—so come prepared!)

Strategy #8: Be Polite, But Advocate for Yourself

Attempt to listen respectfully while being sure to communicate your most important needs and questions.

You may benefit from the following checklist I've created for your initial (first or second) one-on-one meeting with your supervisor. These questions and steps will allow you to learn critical information even if your supervisor isn't being proactive about divulging it.

Template for First One-on-One with Supervisor

This is a time to get to know your supervisor as a person and ask key questions. Consider this as *your* meeting, designed to help you do your job better. Ask or say:

- "I am so excited to be here. I've had a chance to tour the building and meet with some of my new colleagues. I learned this so far:_____ "
- "What is your favorite part of working for this company?"
- "What do you like doing in your off time?" If there are family pictures in the supervisor's workspace, ask (tactfully) about them.
- "Regarding communication—
  - What kind of things do you want me to communicate with you?
  - How often do you wish to have communication?
  - How do you like to be communicated with:
    - Email

- Text
  - Meetings
  - Other?
    - My favorite form of communication is:
      _____."
- "What are your goals for me to accomplish for the first:
  - 30 days
  - 60 days
  - 90 days?"

  Note: Make sure they are SMART goals!

- Determine their best availability: "What is your best day and time for meeting with you or for future one-on-ones?"
- Plan your next meeting: "What is our *next* meeting date?"

Where many managers go wrong is by turning the one-on-one into a micromanagement session. They ask for dates that tasks will be done and updates on progress, and that's all. In the process, they miss a lot of nuances around what the employee might need to perform better or become more engaged in goals. This is why a one-on-one should include the employee's agenda. In fact, after the first one-on-one, the rest should be run by the employee. This is the employee's opportunity to organize their thoughts and needs and communicate them to their supervisor.

Moving forward, the agenda should usually be comprised of four parts, being sure to focus on the parts of goals and tasks that are SMART:

1. **Wins:** *What went well for me since our last meeting?*
2. **Hurdles:** *What do I need assistance with, or in what areas will I be running late?*
3. **Priorities:** *What are the most important things I need to do until our next meeting?*
4. **Career:** *How can I further my career while doing this work?*

This is also a time for the manager to provide assistance and feedback. In this way, one-on-one meetings are the best way to keep everyone on the same page. They are a key tool used in *communications* and *coaching*, which we will dive into next.

Chapter 8

AFTER THE HONEYMOON—ONGOING COMMUNICATIONS

As we've established, one-on-ones are foundational to your ability to coach and communicate. They allow managers to give feedback, which includes expressing appreciation and guiding employees in performance improvement. When done in a timely manner, these sessions allow behaviors to be corrected or reinforced. And they permit employees to ask for clarification in any areas that they find fuzzy.

But there are many opportunities outside of these meetings to ensure everyone is "swimming in the right direction." In this chapter, we'll cover how to engage in effective communications. You'll use these skills in your one-on-ones and beyond.

- If you're a *manager*, it's obvious why communications matter, as no one will know what you expect of them unless you tell them in a way that they understand and respect.
- If you're an *employee*, the strategies in this chapter will give you skills to better relay important details to your manager.

The goal with your communications and coaching is to *bridge the gap* between what a manager expects and what an employee understands and can achieve. In the process, you gain deeper relationships, which leads to higher performance and engagement.

Communications

Communication is the broad umbrella term for how you deliver a message. Simply put, communication involves transferring a message from the giver to the receiver. This includes *mass communications*—such as group emails and media announcements. It also includes *interpersonal communications* between individuals.

Communication can be written and verbal; those forms are obvious. But did you know that 55 percent of communication is nonverbal? The remaining 38 percent is conveyed vocally, and 7 percent of the message comes through the actual words. This analysis was made by Albert Mehrabian, a researcher who studied face-to-face conversation. Specifically, he observed how we pick up conflicting messages between our ears and our eyes (Quinn, 2023).

That means that even if we're not speaking, we're communicating. It could be in our facial expressions, the blocking of our body, or our micro-movements. Often we're not even aware that we're communicating because we're so focused on something else—like thinking about what to say!

For the neurodivergent, communication can be even more challenging.

Clear as Mud

Someone on the spectrum may struggle to read non-verbal cues or nuanced tones of voice. They may take messages literally, based on words-only, thereby missing the subtlety. This is why sarcasm can be so easily misunderstood, because the words don't mean what they say; they usually mean the opposite! Imagine how confusing this is to someone who can't "read" your body language or tone. Not only is the message lost, but the recipient may feel even more like an outsider, especially when they miss an inside joke that the group is bonding over. Humor (jokes) can be similarly misunderstood.

This confusion can also play out when people with some forms of neurodivergence speak. They may not adjust their voice tone or body language to align with our expectations. Effectively, it's almost like they're speaking a different language.

These are some reasons why communications must address the needs of a neurodiverse workforce.

Tied to communications, a recent survey I conducted uncovered some concerning trends that I want to share here on the topic of neurodivergence. The following table shows participants' self-reported responses about how they'd been negatively labeled at work. Note the differences based on gender and whether someone is neurotypical versus neurodiverse.

Neurodivergent Females Who Had Been Called "Aggressive" or "Difficult to Work with"	Neurotypical Females Who Had Been Called "Aggressive" or "Difficult to work with"	Neurodivergent Males Who Had Been Called "Aggressive," "Difficult," or "Unapproachable"	Neurotypical Males Who Had Been Called "Aggressive" or "Unapproachable"
80.95 percent	47.37 percent	85.71 percent	12.5 percent

In summary, this data shows two concerning points:

1. *Neurodivergent* participants were much more likely to be labeled negatively than their *neurotypical* counterparts.
2. *Women* were more likely to be labeled negatively than *men*—and this gap was significantly greater within the two neurotypical groups.

While this was a small study that included more neurodivergent than neurotypical participants, I'd like to expand upon it to see how these trends hold up and what more can be learned. But as a whole, this points to some concerns around how different groups are perceived.

What does this have to do with our communications at work? Perceptions are often formed through communications. They can also be clarified through communications. These are strong motivators for exploring how we can improve our communications strategies within a neurodiverse workplace.

Listen First

Listening is the foundation of communication, and it's closely tied to empathy. Regardless of a neurodivergent diagnosis or situation, most of us could benefit from sharpening our listening skills. Let's explore three reasons why.

Reason #1: Listening Deescalates Conflict

Have you ever butted heads with a partner or friend over something that in retrospect seems so silly, but at the time was something you felt inclined to "go to war" over? As humans, we're prone to react to protect ourselves. This adaptive behavior helps us fend off the fiercest predator. Except that we often misidentify these predators, assuming our spouse is trying to "kill" us (metaphorically), when really they just want to know why we threw our dirty clothes on the bedroom floor … next to the clothes hamper! If we have neurodivergence—especially PTSD from past traumas—our nervous system may be triggered into fight-or-flight mode more quickly than most. Whatever the situation, we can benefit from, and de-fuse a battle by, listening to the other's point of view before reacting with sharpened talons pointed outward.

Reason #2: Listening Helps You Get to Know Someone

Stripe's chief operating officer (and former Google executive leader) Claire Hughes Johnson states, "I always like to know what's going on personally with people so I can see the whole picture. I am a believer that we are 'whole selves,' not work selves and home selves, and it will help me know you and your team better if I know context. If something hard is going on with someone on your team, I'd love to know and be there to support you/them."

Getting to know someone for who they authentically are will build rapport and activate *mirror neurons* that build empathy and engagement. These are brain cells that respond whether we observe an action or do it ourselves. Here's an assignment: Look for signs and key themes that point to the core of the person next to you. With the possible exception of those on the scale of sociopathy, most people give regular signs of their true nature and motivations. While companies often throw around the phrase "wearing many hats," few of us have the ability or desire to shed the "hat" we were born with.

Reason #3: Listening Builds Solutions

If you want to know why your teenager came home sobbing today, don't go ask your elderly neighbor; ask the source. Too often, leaders make the mistake of "fixing" problems without asking the frontline employees who are actually dealing with the issue. This may result in an expensive "fix" that doesn't actually work. I see this often in healthcare, where nurses aren't consulted about policy or procedural changes, and the proposed solutions create more work while compromising patient care. Instead of jumping to changes that won't work, I recommend focus groups with those who might be affected by a change, or two-way improvement teams that involve managers and frontline employees in creating solutions. If one in five of them is neurodivergent, we'll implicitly find solutions for a neurodiverse workforce in this process.

At some point, you've probably heard from a spouse or friend, "Can't you just *listen* to me?" But talk is cheap, as they say; doing it is so much harder. This is why listening is such a hot workplace and leadership topic—considered one of the core tenets of empathy and emotional intelligence. Even with extensive awareness and training, if you put us in a room with an argumentative, triggering, and critical tone, our instincts often lead us to get defensive or go on the attack. That's when we're apt to put our foot in our mouth—or worse yet, use that foot to kick others when they're down.

Most of us aren't great listeners. Even if we're not reacting in anger or irritation, we're easily distracted or amped up, which doesn't suit us when a coworker needs our attention. So now that we know why listening is important, how can we do a better job of it?

Illuminating New Solutions

When my husband, Scott, wasn't putting laundry in the hamper for the umpteenth time, I knew I needed to say something.

"Hey, why are your socks on the floor *again*?" I asked one morning, exasperated. I sort of meant it as a rhetorical question, so it surprised me when he had an actual answer.

"It's because I couldn't see the hamper!" he said simply.

It turns out when I went to sleep and turned the lights out before he came to bed, he couldn't see the laundry receptacle. So we put in a motion activated nightlight that went on when he walked by the hamper, without lighting up the room. He stopped missing the hamper, and I still got to sleep!

I could have thought Scott was lazy or entitled. I could have concluded, *I bet he just wants me to do it for him.* But actually, he was being considerate. When we spoke non-confrontationally about this issue—and I listened—we solved it. Voilà!

When you offer feedback, go into it with a mindset that there's likely a good reason behind the behavior—and an even better solution. It's your job to work with the other person to illuminate it.

Communications Channels: Written Versus Verbal

A *communications channel* is a method by which we transfer a message. Many channels exist—whether to convey written or spoken communication (or some other form). Some channels bombard us with distracting or divisive messages, while others beckon us to clear action.

Most people have a preferred channel—or form of communication—that helps them cut through the "noise." Given employees' diverse preferences, the best managers utilize a variety of channels, especially when communicating crucial messages within a neurodiverse workforce.

Whether you're a manager or employee, take the time to learn about all the communication channels available in your company, which may include town hall meetings, team huddles, one-on-ones, emails, intranet, message boards, announcements over a PA system, social media, or even podcasts. You may even create a new channel! For example, I've seen employees form task forces to compile monthly newsletters as part of a change initiative. These updates keep others abreast of technology changes and more. By communicating with their leaders to collect these updates, these employees also learn about why and how a change is happening.

Especially in times of change, people may need to hear these strategic messages up to seven times before they become internalized (McHarris, 2025). This doesn't mean announcements should be ignored the first time, but as humans, it takes us a while to adapt to change.

See the following guidelines around written and verbal communications.

WRITTEN COMMUNICATIONS GUIDELINES (email, newsletters, social media posts)	VERBAL COMMUNICATIONS GUIDELINES (face-to-face, in meetings)

• Realize that all written communication is discoverable. (Do not write anything you don't want to see on a news feed.)
• Be very clear in the communications about what is needed.
• If you cannot make your message clear in two emails, move to a phone call or meeting.
• If your email wasn't responded to, don't use this as an excuse not to meet a deadline. (Make a phone call or schedule a meeting instead.)
	• Do not interrupt (cut people off).
	• Do not steal other people's ideas. If you notice this happening, return the idea to the person (credit or defer to them).
	• Unless absolutely necessary, avoid the phrases:
	  ▫ "We can't do this."
	  ▫ "This won't work."
	  ▫ "We don't have time."
	• Be positive:
	  ▫ "We can research that."
	  ▫ "I will investigate that."
	  ▫ "I can do this part and look into the other."

Eleven Communications Tips for a Neurodiverse Workforce

Communication, and even listening, don't look the same for everyone. These simple strategies, however, tend to be universally helpful.

Tip #1: Pause

This, and the next point, can be done even before you communicate. If you're going into a potentially challenging coaching session and anticipate it may be challenging, take a few minutes to pause from your current activity. You're probably busy, but I guarantee you can adjust your schedule and find three minutes to pause. This can put you in the right mindset to hear the other person rather than react.

Tip #2: Breathe

Try box breathing. (Breathe in for a count of four, hold your breath for a count of four; breathe out for a count of four, hold your breath for a count of four. Then repeat this cycle for a few minutes. Or find another pattern that works for you.) Numerous research studies have shown the power that intentional breathing has to activate our parasympathetic nervous system and override the adrenaline that hijacks our sense of reason. Meditation may seem hocus pocus, but at its core, it involves breathing.

Tip #3: Ask Questions

If you're tempted to talk too much and push your agenda, consider asking quality questions that elicit content-rich answers. Pretend you're interviewing a potential life partner; what curiosity would you show in your questions? Avoid interrogating people by playing "lawyer ball" where you ask leading questions to trap the other person into a specific, pre-planned answer. Some of the best questions draw out answers beyond just yes and no (although sometimes these simple, direct questions are necessary or helpful too).

Tip #4: Reflect that You've Heard the Other Person

If you've just been told someone is struggling with a task, use empathy statements like, "I understand that you're frustrated with the unclear communications. That must make it hard for you to know what to do next." If someone communicated information that requires collaboration, repeat your understanding of it and ask for verification that you're interpreting their words accurately.

Tip #5: Speak with Kindness as Your Guide

I'm not advising that you come across as wishy-washy just to be "nice," especially while coaching an employee. But even strong correction can be issued assertively, without aggression. If you find yourself slipping toward uncontrolled anger, call for a pause (and breathe).

Tip #6: Don't Push Eye Contact

This probably goes against what you've learned in other communications classes, but someone with ASD may be very uncomfortable with eye contact. If you truly want to tap into their superpowers, you'll need to accept some limitations. There are other ways to communicate and show respect.

Tip #7: Give People Time to Respond

Not everyone is Tigger from *Winnie the Pooh*, bouncing off the walls. Some folks need time for their thoughts to fall into place—like the balls on the Powerball lottery on TV. They may need to let ideas percolate a bit—tossing around in their heads before coalescing into complete thoughts and potential action plans.

Tip #8: Give People Personal Space

If someone feels overwhelmed by close contact, they'll be unable to focus on your words. Back up a bit and assess how they're feeling as you communicate.

Tip #9: Consider Your Physical Movements

Some folks don't like large movements. Massive hand gestures could therefore be distracting or intimidating. I'll admit, I have a hard time not talking with my hands!

So sometimes I hold things while talking, or I draw what I'm thinking while I speak. This helps me keep my hands moving so I don't freak out my coworkers.

Tip #10: Accept and Adapt to Different Styles— Checking in Often for Understanding

Some folks may not be very expressive with their faces, for example. This is great for a poker game but hard when you're trying to gauge how someone is feeling at the office. As a manager, check in with people. Try to do this without making anyone feel self-conscious. "How are you doing this morning?" asked in a genuine way is a good start. "Was my email clear or not?" is a more specific way to check in.

In adapting to styles, some neurodivergent people may need a communications workaround. I once worked for a company that had moved many of their manual processes to automated ones. An employee—who I'll call Max here—had previously been able to complete expense reports and billing on time, but suddenly he was late with both processes. As a result, Max's company credit card was cut off, and HR advised us to put him on a personal improvement plan (PIP). We did not understand how Max had gone from someone who was always on time to someone we might need to let go.

When we met with Max, it was discovered he had dyslexia. Since the other processes he'd used were manual, he'd had assistance completing them. Now that they were automated, Max couldn't receive the same assistance. It's worth noting that Max had not disclosed his dyslexia until this point.

Once we realized the issue, Max's management team made accommodations to conduct some of their training verbally. Max also received assistance with his automated expense reports until he had learned to prepare them error-free. As a result of these adjustments based on Max's best learning style, he was later able to shine in his area of expertise—which was sales.

Tip #11: Provide Time for a Cool-Down When Emotions Get Hot

Most people have a "tell" when they're upset. It may be a raised voice, flailing hands, or a sudden cold expression, depending on whether they go into *fight, flight,* or *freeze* mode. Even if we're aware of how we react, we can still be prone to getting our amygdala hijacked when we're upset, so it's helpful to have an "out" when tempers get hot. Taking a break and agreeing to resume the conversation later is often the best option in this scenario.

Tippy Toe

Some marriage counselors recommend using a "code word" to stop a heated conversation in its tracks. A friend told me hers was "tippy toe," derived from the TV show *Seinfeld* (as an alert to the character, Jerry, that someone was entering the room).

"When either of us say this word, we stop talking, or we completely switch the topic," she said. "But just as key to this process, we always come back to it later—when our emotions aren't running high. This gives us time to think and respond instead of react." Besides reminding them of the comedy show, which prompts them to view the situation more lightly, this also helped each of them be more aware of their own emotions. Knowing they had this temporary "out" allowed them to tune into their words and non-verbal communication.

It's probably not realistic to have a code word like this at work, but you can still practice a pause on conversations that aren't productive due to hot emotions. Consider saying, "Can we break on this conversation for now and come back to it later

this afternoon after we've had a chance to think?"
Then reconvene with a more rational mind for
creating solutions.

Meetings in a Neurodiverse Workplace: Eight Tips to Make Your Sessions Shine

Meetings can present special challenges for neurodivergent employees. For example, it can be hard for someone with ADHD to stay focused, especially in long-winded or dry sessions. Someone with ASD may not feel comfortable addressing a room full of people. Someone with anxiety may struggle to speak out when they have an idea. You get the picture.

The solutions already offered in this book—such as around listening and accommodations—will vastly help your meetings run smoothly. But I'd like to add a few more specific tips here to improve your meetings. As a manager, since you'll never disclose who on your team is neurodiverse or not, these systems will help you maximize all team members.

Tip #1: Ensure that Slides Are Engaging and Informative

Most office employees are familiar with the term "death by PowerPoint." To avoid becoming "bored to death," follow these tips for effective slides.

- Make your slides clear, covering:
- What is the topic?
- What are the findings?
- Make the presentation interesting.
- Use fewer words and fewer slides—but tell a story.
- Tailor the content to the learners.
- Use images, graphics, or charts to help convey your message.
- Create straightforward charts.
- Make data sources simple to follow.

Tip #2: Use Time Limits

A few leaders once approached me, upset. They said one of my direct reports, Sally Sue, had been rude in meetings. I hadn't witnessed it, because I hadn't needed to be in those meetings. So I offered to attend the next session to assess and provide coaching if needed.

After the meeting, I spoke to those who had complained. "How do you feel the meeting went?" I asked.

"It was frustrating. Did you see how Sally Sue is making it so we can't push any ideas forward? We got nothing done!" Their responses echoed each other's.

But I'd observed something different. I'd seen that the folks complaining were cutting off my employee and not allowing her to finish. They were also asserting themselves to complete the task at hand—thereby undermining her autonomy.

"I hear you," I said, "but I observed something else. I saw that Sally wasn't able to finish a sentence or complete her presentation due to interruptions." I provided four concrete examples when these leaders had derailed the meeting, and my employee had tried to get them back on track.

A light bulb went off over these leaders' heads, and we brainstormed a new meeting format to address their frustrations and circumvent their desire to cut her off. We decided to institute a shorter presentation deck with a summary up front, so they could get to the discussion earlier. We also got a koosh ball to pass around when someone was speaking, so there would be no interrupting. And finally, we placed a time limit on Sally's presentation and the responses to it. Who wouldn't benefit from taking turns and making a meeting more concise?

I spoke with Sally to explain the situation, and she agreed that it was frustrating not to be making progress. She also agreed to try the new technique.

After the next two meetings, I requested feedback from the same leaders. Suddenly, my lead was called *proactive, polite,* and *a leader.* She was never again labeled as *rude.*

Time limits and boundaries around speaking can go a long way to empowering voices without drowning out others—or causing them to tune out.

Tip #3: Make Toys Accessible During Meetings

A VP I knew came to my office every week for a call. He couldn't sit still, so he took my Post-It notes and a marker and drew. He knew his own challenges and came equipped to focus on the call.

For other employees, I would keep flexible toys on my desk including a Gumby, a Pokey, and a Lucy doll from *Peanuts.* I found bringing these toys to longer meetings or calls helped team members focus.

Tip #4: Collect Input Before the Meeting

Sometimes introverts—or those who are neurodivergent—have the greatest ideas. But if they never feel empowered or able to speak up—or if they can't communicate clearly when they do—you'll never know. One way to gather and amplify their thoughts is to ask for input—potentially ideas or challenges to address—before the meeting. Someone can then be in charge of collecting this input and building it into the agenda.

I once managed an employee who was slow at processing but also very bright. I gave him access to materials ahead of time, so he could synthesize the information and gather his feedback. He couldn't digest on the fly during the meeting, but his input was highly valuable.

Sometimes I would also meet one-on-one with an employee prior to the meeting, and then again after, to get their thoughts. This helped those who struggled to speak publicly, because they still got a chance to communicate.

Tip #5: Disperse an Agenda Ahead of Time

Employees should receive the agenda at least twenty-four hours before the meeting, so they have time to digest it and form questions or content to share.

Tip #6: Communicate about Important Changes/ Issues Ahead of Time

Some issues are particularly sensitive and deserve special attention before a larger group meeting. Use discretion about who needs to know what, and when.

I once spoke to a manager about how his team reacted to the changes announced in larger leadership meetings. "They're like thoroughbred horses!" he said of his employees. "They're great when they can be free. If you put them in a stall, they become mean!" Instead of unleashing these "horses" in the larger meetings, the manager got permission to give certain sales reps a heads up prior to the release of new changes. This allowed them to let off steam before the bigger announcements.

Change Management

Change can be very hard for anyone, and especially for some neurodivergent people. Whenever possible, bringing some frontline employees into the change process will also allow them to be part of the transformation. They may become champions, spreading the benefits to other employees who don't yet know why things must change. Communicating early and often is the best change management strategy to keep people from derailing a new initiative.

Tip #7: Get Moving

This won't work for everyone or in every setting (and, once again, should *not* be required since some people aren't able to move in this way), but one senior leader I knew used to take employees on a walk around the office—or even to a nearby park—to discuss important topics. For kinesthetic learners or those with hyperactivity or attention challenges, this can help ideas percolate and stick. This only would be done *after* you get to know someone's preferred style.

Communication can be challenging in the best of circumstances, which is why it's something to practice repeatedly. But doing it effectively will help you bridge the gap between employees, including between the neurodiverse and neurotypical. I hope that the strategies in this chapter have equipped you to transfer your knowledge and ideas to others respectfully and effectively in your neurodiverse workplace.

Communication is also foundational to *coaching*, which we will cover in the next chapter.

Chapter 9

COACHING—THE FOUNDATION OF ALL PERFORMANCE

Throughout this book, I've stressed the importance of treating each person on the team as an individual. However, as much as we need to meet someone where they are, it's also important to hold everyone to the same high expectations and performance evaluations. And the way this is done is through coaching.

Coaching is closely tied to communications. It's a simple concept: Coaching involves providing *feedback* so that someone knows what you're thinking and what you expect.

If you want a workplace that fosters performance and engagement, coaching is your most critical tool. While it all hinges around the one-on-ones, which we already covered, several additional coaching principles are critical in the process. We'll explore them in this chapter.

Start with the Positive

While we think of feedback as negative, the best managers provide sufficient positive coaching to reinforce the right behaviors—in other words, praising someone for a job well done. Then, when that person needs corrective feedback, it can be done from an existing foundation of mutual trust and respect. Not only does this foster feel-good chemicals like oxytocin that bond us to one another and deepen our relationships, but it also clearly spotlights what you want someone to do.

Employees are not dogs, but bear with me while I use this example. Because at our core, some of the same behavioral truths apply. That is, when trainers try to teach a dog to sit, they don't punish the dog for not sitting. Instead, they give it a treat when it sits. In no time, Fido becomes so eager for the treat that he is looking into your eyes and waiting for your command, as his drool begins to stream in anticipation of the salmon snack.

For a human example, recall my husband putting laundry into the basket. Had we not found a simple solution of illuminating the hamper area, the next best option would have been to catch my husband getting it right. A leader once told me, "If you want your spouse to put the clothes in the hamper more often, praise them the next time they put their clothes in the hamper."

As humans, we're drawn toward appreciation. Many large studies repeatedly show this, sometimes ranking appreciation above items related to pay or promotion.

Consider once again how an athletic coach operates. When a runner is training for a marathon, their coach gives them a specific training plan and then monitors their progress. Along the way, the coach cheers on the runner who executes a solid workout, telling them specifically what they're doing well: "Great job keeping your pace on target during your tempo run!" By establishing that positive reinforcement loop, the coach can also offer feedback on what to change: "Next time, try increasing your cadence by shortening your stride and taking more steps per minute." This leads to a celebration when the finish line is crossed—a joint effort made possible by solid coaching and strong execution.

Six Steps for Providing Corrective Feedback

The best ongoing coaching plans include *praise*, *plans*, and *pointed direction* to guide someone on their course. This is done through one-on-ones as well as informal feedback.

This feedback may address tasks that need to get done, strategic goals to attain, or interpersonal issues that must be resolved.

Once you've established a positive relationship, you'll have an easier time giving corrective feedback. This should be seen as a constructive and good thing since it allows an employee to be part of their own success story.

Missed Promotion

Going back to my husband's missed promotion in his first year out of school, had his manager been meeting with Scott weekly and providing feedback about his office demeanor, Scott could have fixed it early. Instead, his manager waited until the end of the year when it was too late for Scott to make corrections, and the promotion was lost. Scott also had to rebuild the relationship between himself and the group that perceived him poorly. Instead of having one or two bad interactions, he needed to atone for a year's worth of bad behavior. This was a much steeper uphill climb. My well-meaning husband had to wait another year for that promotion.

Coaching should happen regularly, using the one-on-one as your primary method.

Following are six steps to follow when giving feedback. Rather than force yourself to follow them in order—although they do work progressively as outlined here—consider them as fundamental guidelines to follow.

Step #1: Find a Timely Opportunity to Share Your Feedback

Don't wait until bad behaviors get entrenched or good behaviors get ignored. Tell the person what you see now—or as close to when it happens as you can. This might be through an informal conversation on your way to lunch if it's something minor, or a scheduled meeting if it's more complex.

Step #2: Focus on the Problem Behavior—Not the Person—and Convey the Specific Impact on Them and Others

This is the part that requires some thinking and planning, since it's easy to react poorly when someone isn't doing what we want.

Here's an example to help us explore this. Let's say Donald is disrupting your team meetings by constantly interjecting before anyone can finish. You see that other group members are irritated, and it's hard to make progress on hearing their updates, let alone getting to the planning stage. If you were focused on Donald and how he's acting as a person, you might be tempted to say, "You have a bad attitude," or "You're so disrespectful." But what does a *bad attitude* or *disrespect* actually look like? The problem with saying this—besides the fact that it may come across as inflammatory and triggering—is that it's not specific. Thus, it's not clear. Donald is more apt to be hurt or mad than motivated and equipped to change.

I'm not suggesting that you need to smother all negative feelings about an employee's behavior. That frustration is probably what's driving you to seek a change, so the emotion serves a purpose! But to be effective in your coaching, you should focus on *observable behaviors* that are clear and fact-based. And you should try not to let your emotions curtail that communication.

You might say something like this: "Donald, I noticed you interrupted other team members in our meeting today when they were trying to update everyone on the software integration. This made it hard to get the updates we need from each person on the project, and we ran out of time for anyone to ask you questions about your data. Our project won't be done on time if this continues, and if you want to be given higher-stakes projects, this needs to change." By being specific about what you saw and

why it matters to Donald, the team, and the organization, he knows what behavior he needs to change.
As you describe the problem, here are some
clarifying tips:

- **Be specific.** Focus on breaking down tasks and
  instructions to be as straightforward and simple
  as possible, emphasizing the behaviors you're
  trying to discourage or encourage. Explain how
  their actions impact the people they interact
  with, including team members, customers, and
  other stakeholders.
- **Include examples.** Avoid generalities; instead
  share specific scenarios.
- **Include how something makes you feel
  using "I feel," "I saw," and "I think…"**
- **Ask if there was another way the person
  could have handled it.** This gives them a chance
  to reflect and come up with their own solutions.

Step #3: Offer an Example of the Behavior or Change You Want to See, Explaining the Benefit to Them and Others

You might say, "As I've shared, interrupting disrupts
our progress and frustrates others. If you want to meet

your goal of advancing in our company, I'd like to see you wait until others are finished talking. This shows that you're listening and allows us to learn from each other. You can use a parking lot for any ideas that you're afraid you'll forget. That way, we can get to the testing phase and go live with our new software by our goal date. I also think this will help you get along better with your teammates."

As you come up with solutions, build on the employee's strengths. If you know they struggle in one area, provide extra support. If you know they shine in another, give them opportunities to work more in that area.

Step #4: Ask The Employee to Repeat Back Their Understanding of the Issue and Its Solution, and Resolve Any Outstanding Obstacles

Ask them to repeat back their understanding of the issue and potential solutions. Close any gaps in expectations. This is critical because it's all too common to talk "at" an employee rather than "with" them. Nothing gets solved if they don't understand your expectations and feel equipped to meet them.

Step #5: Provide Opportunities to Practice Getting It Right

If your team needs help in a particular area, set up meetings where they can practice these skills through role plays. If it's just one person, have them practice with you. When I worked for Perot Systems, an information technology service provider, we did quarterly management retreats, and most of the day was spent practicing difficult conversations. This included topics like:

- How to give positive and negative feedback
- How to coach a team
- Change management

Practicing these skills in a safe space made it easier when we finally had to use them.

Step #6 (Ongoing): Reinforce Positive Behavioral Modification with Generous Praise

Just like houseplants, employees grow toward the light. Besides giving positive words up front, use them as a tool to reinforce behavioral changes. Some models suggest that to truly motivate employees in the right behaviors, the ratio of positive to negative feedback should be five to one or greater. And in times of change, that positive reinforcement should increase.

Closely tied to this is *recognition*. A 2014 study conducted of 200,000 people by BCG found that of many factors, the most important component to employees is that they experience *appreciation* at work (Strack et al., 2021). Especially for neurodivergent employees who've heard their share of negative words said about them—such as "aggressive" or "difficult to work with," as detailed in the last chapter—offering them generous appreciation is an investment well made. Find ways to reinforce and recognize them regularly, showing your appreciation. This can be through formal programs coordinated with HR, or it can occur in your informal, kind words of recognition.

As you get to know someone, you'll be able to figure out what works best for them in terms of recognition and motivation. Again, note that your feedback shouldn't be generic, like, "Good job, whatever your name is. I'm sure you'll do well at your next event, whatever that is." Instead, coaching feedback is specific, and it requires a relationship where two people with common goals develop mutual respect as they work together. To reinforce this concept, this chart shows some examples of statements that provide effective and behavior-focused feedback:

OBSERVED PROBLEM STATEMENT	POSSIBLE SOLUTION STATEMENT
"I noticed in our meeting that you responded quickly to the customer with a 'no' response."	"It would be more helpful to our customers to say, 'We will look into it' or 'We may not be able to do all of that, but we will see what we can provide.'"
"I've noticed that this report contains this same error each month."	• "Is your spreadsheet formatted correctly?" • "Do you need help understanding the report and what we are looking for?" • "Is there additional training I can provide?"
"Great job on that report."	"That report you provided made it very clear to the team which answer we should choose."
"The team appreciated the presentation you put together."	"Your presentation was well organized and had all the data we needed to guide the committee to a decision. Thank you."

Again, coaching doesn't always need to be formal. If you catch an employee in the hallway and recall something amazing they did in the meeting that morning, call them out on it. It can be as simple as: "Hey, Shirley. That question you asked in today's meeting about our AI chat tool was incredibly effective in moving us toward a better solution on the customer service initiative. Keep it up." Note how this is positive and specific.

Addressing—and Ultimately Preventing—Mistakes

It's unrealistic to expect that mistakes won't happen. Coaching should include a process whereby employees can address their mistakes.

- As a manager, allow for mistakes. Then look for ways to correct them. People learn from mistakes.
- As an employee, realize that everyone makes mistakes. This doesn't make you a failure.

While those statements are true and helpful, I'm also not suggesting you use them as excuses to permit ongoing, unchecked errors. For one, mistakes don't always *need* to happen. The best way to avoid them is to equip employees to ask questions. By involving the employee in finding the answer, it forces them to put some thought and effort into the answer before asking the question. Over time, an employee can develop increased autonomy around decision-making as their critical thinking expands with their experience.

To this end, I train my employees to communicate their questions or "grey areas" in one of these three ways:

1. **Ask for help:** "I looked in the SOP documents, and I can't figure out the next step. Would it be possible for you to walk me through it?"

   □ This shows the lowest level of autonomy, as the employee needs to know: *What do I need to do in this situation?*

2. **Ask for approval:** "I looked through the SOP and did some additional research. I believe that the next step I should take is this one. Are you okay with that?"

   □ This shows more independence and confidence (and presumably competence).

3. **State your plan:** "We've run into this issue, and I will be taking these steps unless you have any concerns."

   □ This really isn't a question. It represents a high level of autonomy and communicates: *I am doing this unless you tell me not to.*

After this, I don't expect them to come back with questions on this same topic. They may, however, come to me with new questions showing that they've made some effort to apply their knowledge gained.

POOR QUESTIONS SHOW:	BETTER (GOOD) QUESTIONS SHOW:
• No reflection on past directions • No initiative taken thus far • No brainstorming on options • No gratitude or respect for the person's time	• Evidence of listening to one's manager and peers • Completion of some research on the topic • Attention paid during training • An effort to learn the organization and who knows what • Ideas about possible solutions • Gratitude for the assistance

Even when an employee doesn't initially know what to do, I expect them to take some initiative to help their manager navigate the task. Along these lines, I once managed a senior analyst, Angela, who sent the following email to three directors:

Good morning,

The customer just sent us the email below, stating that the language we quoted is not in their agreement. How would you like me to respond?

—Angela

Her email didn't follow any of the three guidelines. It didn't show any research done or initiative taken. Considering that Angela had been with us for more than a year and was at a senior level, her passive approach concerned me.

When I coached Angela, I explained that I would have preferred her to send something like:

Good morning,

The customer just sent us the email below, stating that the language we quoted is not in their agreement. I researched the contract, and the language is in Section 5, which I'm also pasting below. Please let me know if you want me to respond or if one of you will respond.

—Angela

Encouraging your employees' autonomy to research and brainstorm options will help them feel more comfortable in their roles while eventually minimizing errors. With neurodivergent employees who may have experienced a lack of trust in their skills, this also builds confidence where it may have been previously lacking.

Managing Up: Providing Feedback to Your Boss

Feedback isn't given just from a manager to an employee. As an employee, this is often referred to as "managing up," since you're enabling yourself to perform better while clarifying what you need from them. Saying something like, "The way you provided the information for this project was very helpful, and it made getting it done much easier," will help to inform and encourage a manager in the style that works best for you.

Managing up also can be done when your boss does something that doesn't work for you. If you need something presented or done in a different way, it's on you to ask for it—respectfully, of course. For example, if you struggle to track verbally, consider saying, "I have an easier time following directions when they're written. Would you mind sending me a list of the tasks you need from me, or allowing me to take notes while you dictate them to me?"

Or perhaps your boss is neurodivergent, and they struggle to understand your communications or even motivations. You may need to clarify details with them about the task at hand—or even to clear the air. The latter has happened to me!

I once had a boss, let's call him Sven, who was considered to be "difficult." He would give conflicting orders—telling one person something and me another. I often found myself in between Sven and others who were trying to interpret his instructions. So I would ask a *lot* of clarifying questions of Sven to be sure I understood his desires.

Then one day, Sven grew very frustrated with me. He began to avoid me—not answering emails or his phone, not addressing me during meetings, and not scheduling any one-on-ones. This went on for a couple of months.

Then one day, Sven showed up and needed to make a private phone call in my office. After he was done, I came back in and asked him if I could talk to him about something. He had no way out of the conversation since I was between him and the door. (I'm not recommending that you physically block your boss, but this is just how it turned out!) This was my chance to speak.

"It feels clear to me that I've upset you in some way, and it's negatively impacting our work relationship." I waited for a response.

Sven, of course, denied being upset—while looking around the room, trying to find an escape from this dreaded conversation. There were no windows to jump out of.

I shared specific examples of why I felt Sven was upset with me. "This is impacting not just our relationship, but my ability to run my region," I said directly.

After much input by me, Sven got so upset that he finally blurted out, "You always question my authority by asking a million questions!"

I sat down in my chair and proceeded to explain to my boss that I respected his authority, but I didn't always understand what he wanted from me. "I need more information to carry out your instructions, hence the questions," I explained.

This led to a productive conversation, which was a pivotal point in our relationship. He eventually understood my motivation, and I think we both felt our interactions became much more positive after that day.

If I hadn't addressed this tension with my boss, he never would have divulged what was at the root of it. Confrontation was a huge source of stress for him. By managing up to him in this way, we avoided a lot of future friction. Over the next few years, there were some times when I needed to speak my truth again, pushing back against his directives. But once he knew I didn't question his authority, he was more willing to listen to a conflicting idea, or to agree to disagree.

If you see something that needs to be addressed with your boss, use the communication and coaching (including one-on-one) skills in this book. This is how you bridge gaps and pave the way for a smoother future.

Eight Tactical Tips to Help Your Neurodiverse Workforce Perform at Their Best

We've already established that neurodivergent people come with some incredible strengths. We've also explored the limitations when someone struggles to focus, make eye contact, or interpret nuanced language. Here are some additional, more tactical tips that can help a neurodiverse workforce achieve goals and contribute positively to the team and their own career. Some of these have already been touched on throughout this book, but I'm targeting them here in a more specific way so you can prioritize them in your coaching.

Tip #1: Break Down Tasks into Smaller Pieces, Using Checklists and Bullet Points

Data dumps can be overwhelming, but task lists with subtasks beneath them can provide clarity and encourage progress. The same concept applies to large goals; break them up into measurable pieces with a checklist. Don't be afraid to include easy stuff to give a sense of gratification when it's done. Have you ever created a list of tasks and included things you've already done, just so you can cross them off? It's reinforcing to see progress in this way!

Tip #2: Use a Parking Lot Technique

This can be useful in meetings when someone has an idea at a time when it's inappropriate to talk about it. That thought can sit there—like a Subaru in a parking lot—until it's time to rev it up, and it won't disappear. Encourage employees to write down notes and questions, and then include a time in your meeting at the end to address these. If a topic needs more follow-up, schedule a one-on-one. As an employee, you can proactively do this even if your manager doesn't offer a formal parking lot. This is especially helpful for people with ADHD who might otherwise be tempted to interrupt in order not to forget a thought.

Tip #3: Check in for Understanding

You must be sure someone understands directions, because that's not a given. As I've shared before, asking them to repeat what they understand goes a long way. Apply this in a multitude of settings to improve performance and relationships.

Tip #4: Understand That Self-Esteem Issues May Be at Play

Neurodivergent people often deal with a lot of criticism and perceived failure. Be sensitive to this when you provide and ask for information. You don't need to walk on eggshells, but you do need to show empathy.

Tip #5: Suggest Time Blocking

Organizing a schedule to meet a work goal can feel overwhelming to someone who struggles with time management or executive functioning. Helping someone by providing a schedule of when to work on which tasks can help them accomplish a lot more.

Tip #6: Consider Using a Coach Who Specializes in Helping Neurodivergent People

This is an area I work in, as I've shared, and I've seen firsthand what a difference it can make.

Budgeting for Life

I recently coached a gentleman with ASD who had time management issues. His supervisor knew he should be a top performer. He had transferred from another research project where he had done excellent work.

But as a member of the local research team, he was struggling to keep up with his monthly deadlines and work with his colleagues. His manager was doing everything correctly by having one-on-ones and checking on his priorities. But his coworkers were getting frustrated by his questions, and progress was stalling. He was referred to me for coaching.

During his first session, we discovered that part of his job involved "firefighting" issues for the team during the day. Because he was so good at certain tasks, he was constantly interrupted by various people wanting him to do something "small"—"really quickly." Those tasks added up, and he was unable to focus on his other deadlines.

As his coach, I asked if these "fires" would shut down the department. "Or could they wait?" I questioned.

He said they could wait.

"How many fires do you deal with on an average day?" I asked.

He didn't know, so we decided to have him place all the "distractions" on a parking lot list.

The thinking was that he could get to them after he'd completed work on the higher priorities.

But first, this needed to be discussed with his manager. That meeting—and the parking lot he showed her—proved pivotal because the manager now had sightlines to all the other items that had become issues in her department.

Currently, my client emails this list to his manager at the end of each day. She then lets him know which tasks can wait, so he can continue to focus on his key priorities. This is an example of how a coach who is versed with neurodivergence can help to create breakthroughs.

Tip #7: Have Reasonable Expectations around Social Interaction

"Jackson doesn't go to lunch with us, so he must not like us." I've heard this from team members about a neurodivergent person who prefers to eat alone. We need to respect people's personal energy and the time it takes them to recharge. We may not know who is neurodivergent or neurotypical, but it's okay to let someone read a book or listen to music at lunch, especially if their job requires meetings or phone work all day.

On the flip side, I've also coached introverted or neurodivergent clients to help them find the energy to socialize once in a while. I might advise: "Find a quiet moment in your day to recharge, so you can go for a drink or appetizer after work. Socializing is an expected part of the job. And when you do go out, try not to talk about work. This is an opportunity to get to know your coworkers. Listen to them and ask about their hobbies." Sometimes I make this into a game with a deal like:

- *If I go out twice in a month, then I can stay in and watch Netflix with my dogs over a weekend.*

Or:

- *If I network for my job this week, then I get a prize.*

Tip #8: Know When to Move People

As a manager, you may find that an employee just isn't fitting into the role you originally hired them for. Or you may discover a hidden talent in someone that you didn't know about during their recruitment. If I find that an employee has a particular strength I need, I might move them into a different position if I can. (Keep in

mind, it's helpful to move folks around equitably—
allowing anyone the chance to advance into greater
roles and responsibility within their strengths.) And if an
employee struggles in one area, I try to find somewhere
they shine before dismissing them altogether.

I once had a team member, Lanette, who was awful
at handling the sales force but wonderful at writing SOPs.
Her peers were falling behind on other work because
they hated writing SOPs and peer audits. No one on
my team had disclosed being neurodivergent, but as
a manager, I still needed to understand my team's needs
and strengths. So I moved the SOPs and audits to Lanette
and removed sales calls from her workload.

"I love it!" Lanette later told me. She was happy,
and the others were relieved to lose this part of their
daily tasks.

I won't go into depth about how to let someone go
who isn't working out. But I will say this typically happens
when coaching is no longer helping an employee stay
at the minimum standard required for their role—or
ideally, above that. If moving them around isn't possible
or doesn't help, it may be time to have that discussion.
It's not a step to take lightly, so involve HR to ensure
it's done legally and ethically. You will need a lot of documentation and likely a performance improvement plan

(PIP) along the way before moving on to this decision. If you've been doing regular one-on-ones, providing clear feedback, and offering additional training and assistance as needed—with clear documentation along the way—a dismissal should not come as a surprise to the employee. Likewise, their performance review, whether good or bad, should never be a surprise.

Coaching doesn't resolve every problem, but it's the best way to guide people into their best performance and role based on their strengths, style, and preferences. After reading this chapter, I hope you feel more equipped to coach—or be coached—to maximize engagement for the whole team.

Conclusion

BRIDGING THE GAPS
AS THEY COME

Throughout this book, I've likened employees to fish in the sea, trying to navigate and find their pod where they can function, move forward, and thrive. Without mixing metaphors, I now want to use one that guides my coaching (and is part of the title of this book): *bridging the gap*.

As a manager, I believe that you have a unique perspective to view the "fishes of the sea" and see how they operate. From your perspective "on the bridge," you can make changes that help employees "swim straighter" or "find their pod." The purpose of this book has been to give you that perspective, so that you can step back and find solutions you might not see when you're in the thick of it.

While this applies to managers, it also works for employees. I hope that this perspective has equipped you with more tools and better strategies to understand yourself and others. And I especially hope that this aids you in reaching your wildest goals.

If you follow all the principles in this book, besides understanding yourself and others better, you'll be well on your way to creating a better environment in which to thrive. Essentially, all of these ideas will help you bridge gaps between the neurodivergent and neurotypical—creating an engaged, high-performing "sea" in which to thrive. I hope you can appreciate the diversity you see and let it guide you to new and better places.

In closing, I want to leave you with a few final over-arching strategies that will help you bridge any remaining or ongoing gaps—again and again, as they arise. Because as we all know, the workplace is a dynamic environment, just like our world. Both are always changing, and it's up to us to choose how we will respond.

Strategy #1: Focus on the Principles that Are Most Critical to You and Your Team

As you reflect back on what you've read in this book, consider integrating the most crucial principles into your coaching plans. If *listening* is a key trait you want to see more of, for example, build it into your performance evaluations and provide regular feedback on how someone is doing. But don't wait until their annual reviews (which are quickly falling out of favor in many large companies) to let them know their status; coach continuously, so there are no surprises. Whatever principles or strategies seem most crucial to you right now—which might be the ones that are tripping you up the most—are the ones you should prioritize first. Over time, you can add more.

Strategy #2: Model the Desired Skills

If you're a parent to young children, you know how modeling works. Your toddler is watching you, looking for behaviors to emulate. (Once they're teenagers, they hope to do the opposite of you, so take advantage of this window when they're young! Yes, that's meant to be a joke—sort of.) Similarly, in the workplace, leaders walk around with a spotlight on their heads, hands, and hearts. The best way to instill a behavior in employees is to emulate it. Want better written communications? Brush up on your writing skills, and use an editor if necessary before blasting out emails with typos. Want better conflict resolution? Practice the "pause and breathe" technique before spouting off at a manager within earshot of their staff. As the famous Ghandi quote states, "Be the change you want to see in the world." Whether you're an executive leader or frontline employee, you have the opportunity to lead yourself—modeling all the attributes you want to see more of.

Strategy #3: Cultivate Allies

Most fish don't swim alone. And even if they do, they're part of a diverse ecosystem that includes adversaries. Because of that, they also need allies, especially if they're outnumbered. When conflict arises in an environment—like a storm that makes the water seem particularly murky—we may even need to help each other find a way to safety where we can thrive.

As we navigate this ocean of diverse fish that is our workplace, here are some closing thoughts to help ensure your team is swimming in unison, promoting allies instead of adversaries.

Educate Yourself

Read about the history of systemic inequality, immerse yourself in stories of people who have different backgrounds and experiences than yourself, and actively work to diversify your networks. Allyship shouldn't end with increasing your knowledge, but it is an important place to start.

Resist Assuming What Others Need

One size does not fit all. In an age that is influenced by whatever is shiny and grabs our attention on social media, it's important to remind ourselves that we don't always know what a person thinks—or needs—until we ask them. And we cannot assume that each person needs the same type of allyship.

Listen Deeply

We must identify what is going on around us in order to spotlight the issue. Being an ally does not involve merely asking a person, "How can I help you?" We must listen in a broader sense, watch what's happening, and become more aware of our surroundings. And then we must respond accordingly to what we hear and see with sensitivity.

Don't Put People into Boxes

Everyone has their own past experiences that shape what they need. We're not just one identity. We can be female, married, six feet tall, Jewish, white, older, with children, with ADD, and more. Employees want to be able to bring their whole selves to work, to do their best job possible. Give others the freedom to be who they are, and try to find that freedom for yourself.

Recognize That Privilege Is Power

Privilege can come from having a college education or being able-bodied, neurotypical, male, or white. Someone who isn't in these categories may be working very hard while still swimming against a strong and established current.

Don't Let Fear of Saying the Wrong Thing Keep You from Trying

Many people, especially those in a majority group, may be so afraid of saying or doing the wrong thing that they do nothing at all. But inaction and silence are harmful too. Give yourself, and each other, some grace for making missteps.

Whether you're neurodivergent or neurotypical, you're one fish in a greater pod that is hopefully swimming toward the next shiny goal. With the right tools in place, you can shine like one of those superstars covered early in this book.

Going back to another early example, my son, who once struggled to communicate—and then became diagnosed with ASD—is now a thriving biomedical engineer. He learned how to lean into his strengths, advocate for himself, and get where he needed to be. And he was fortunate to have some professors and managers who knew how to mentor him along the way.

Like my family members and so many whom I have coached, my goal for you after reading this book is that you walk away realizing these truths:

- As an employee, your neurodivergence doesn't need to isolate you. In fact, it can fuel your success.
- As a manager, your employees' neurodiversity doesn't need to derail your progress. In fact, it can drive your team to explore new worlds and achieve more than you imagined.

Whatever your role, I hope you now feel more equipped to make these truths a reality in the "ocean" of your workplace. And I hope you feel more empowered in your unique strengths.

Acknowledgments

As I've mentioned, writing has always been challenging for me. I've started and stopped this book countless times because the process of sitting still, reflecting on the hardships my family and I have overcome, and striving to articulate the right words to convey key training concepts took time and effort. But I couldn't be happier with the outcome. This book wouldn't be here without my incredible village who has supported my career, my dreams, and my children's education throughout the years. I'd like to use these final pages to express my gratitude to a few of those people.

I'm especially grateful for my children's special education teachers (especially Sue Silver!). They taught my family what it means to be neurodivergent and helped us build our toolkits and boundaries. Because of them, we learned to openly discuss our experiences, which has allowed us to thrive.

I'm also deeply indebted to my book launch team: my editor, Jocelyn Carbonara; my project manager,

Jenny Lisk; and my designer, George Stevens. They took my ideas and helped me transform them into this book and a business plan. They have expertly channeled my ADHD anxieties into a clear, actionable vision.

To my favorite workplace managers, Terry Lee and William Stewart, thank you for recognizing my skills while demonstrating what a leader should be. You took the time to coach me, which enabled me to leverage my neurodiversity as a strength rather than seeing it as a limitation. I was able to perform at high levels because you gave me the space and tools to do so.

To the employees who worked for me—including Serena Forde, Donna Sessums, Sherry Lund, and the rest of the teams at Perot Systems and DePuy Spine—thank you for teaching me what you needed to succeed and for helping me provide it.

To my support network—Deb Mandell, Jill Levine, Donna Cohen-Avery, Barbara Shays, Carrie Kellerman, Sammi Robertson, and Eileen Kravitz—thank you for listening to my work stories, helping me brainstorm solutions without judgment, and reviewing my book draft. And thank you for supporting my career transition into coaching.

To Joe Rotella and the team at Delphi Consulting, thank you for your support while working with me on webinars and for introducing me to the Society for Human Resource Management (SHRM).

To all the coaches at AANE who have provided me with the opportunity to move into coaching as my next career, I've loved sharing our stories and support during clinical hour, skill building workshops, and even over coffee.

A special thank you to Emily and Andy Moroney, my extended family. We have learned so much together about neurodiversity and our children, recognizing that each autistic individual is unique.

Finally, to my husband, Scott; my mom, Marilyn; and my children, Rachael and Seth; thank you for your unwavering support as we learned, made mistakes, and navigated our diagnoses. To my son and daughter, I'm grateful that you've allowed me to be your mom, coach, and friend, and I'm especially grateful that you've let me share your experiences in this book in order to help others.

References

Anderson, Bruce. "Gallup Suggests That Employee Turnover in U.S. Businesses Is a $1 Trillion Problem—With a Simple Fix," April 25, 2019. https://www.linkedin.com/business/talent/blog/talent-engagement/employee-turnover-in-us-business-is-1-trillion-dollar-problem.

Austin, Robert and Gary Pisano. *Harvard Business Review.* "Neurodiversity as a Competitive Advantage," May 1, 2017. https://hbr.org/2017/05/neurodiversity-as-a-competitive-advantage.

BCG Global. "More Than a Quarter of Employees Globally Are Ready to Move on From Their Current Jobs," n.d. https://www.bcg.com/press/18december2023-employees-move-on-from-current-jobs.

Birch, Kate. "Top 7 companies hiring and nurturing neurodiverse talent." *Business Chief.* Accessed November 23, 2021. https://businesschief.com/human-capital/top-7-companies-hiring-and-nurturing-neurodiverse-talent.

Christ, Ginger. "Half of Neurodivergent Workers
    Say They Want to Quit Their Jobs—or Already
    Have." *HR Dive*, April 5, 2023. https://www.hrdive.
    com/news/half-of-neurodivergent-workers-want-to-
    quit-their-jobs-or-already-have/646889.

Collins, James Charles. *Good to Great: Why Some Companies
    Make the Leap—and Others Don't*. Random House, 2001.

Dennison, Kara. "Gallup Says $8.8 Trillion Is the True
    Cost of Low Employee Engagement." *Forbes*, July
    16, 2024. https://www.forbes.com/sites/karaden-
    nison/2024/07/16/gallup-says-88-trillion-is-the-
    true-cost-of-low-employee-eng
    agement.

Draper, Jessica Jane. "Successful People with Neuro-
    divergent Disabilities—Student News." *Student
    News—News, Information, and Events for Your
    Student Life*. (blog), August 20, 2024. https://
    studentnews.manchester.ac.uk/2024/03/18/
    successful-people-with-neurodivergent-disabilities.

Gallup, Inc. "Learn About the History of Clifton-
    Strengths." Gallup.com, December 17, 2024. https://
    www.gallup.com/cliftonstrengths/en/253754/
    history-cliftonstrengths.aspx.

Gatta, Mary, Ph.D., Joshua Kahn Ph.D., Andrea J. Koncz, Angelena Galbraith, Mabel Sabogal Ph.D., Anna Longenberger, and NACE Research Staff. "Job Outlook 2024." https://www.naceweb.org/docs/default-source/default-document-library/2023/publication/research-report/2024-nace-job-outlook.pdf.

Hansen, Michael. "The U.S. Education System Isn't Giving Students What Employers Need." *Harvard Business Review*, May 18, 2021. https://hbr.org/2021/05/the-u-s-education-system-isnt-giving-students-what-employe rs-need.

Harris, John. "The Mother of Neurodiversity: How Judy Singer Changed the World." *The Guardian*, July 5, 2023. https://www.theguardian.com/world/2023/jul/05/the-mother-of-neurodiversity-how-judy-singer-changed-the-world.

Heinze, Carolyn. "6 Challenges of AI in Recruitment." *Search HR Software*, August 7, 2023. https://www.techtarget.com/searchHRSoftware/feature/Challenges-of-AI-in-recruitment.

McDowall, Almuth; Nancy Doyle; and Meg Kisleva, 2023. "Neurodiversity at Work: Demand, Supply and a Gap Analysis." Birkbeck, University of London, London, UK.

McHarris, Neely. "5 Steps to Better Change Management Communication + Template." Prosci (blog), March 27, 2025. https://www.prosci.com/blog/change-management-communication.

"Martin E.P. Seligman | Positive Psychology Center," n.d. https://ppc.sas.upenn.edu/people/martin-ep-seligman.

Miller, Rachel, PhD. "Top Companies Hiring Neurodivergent Employees." BestColleges.com, August 23, 2023. https://www.bestcolleges.com/careers/companies-hiring-neurodivergent-employees.

Nelson, Bailey. "CliftonStrengths Combinations: Most Rare and Common." Gallup.com, December 26, 2024. https://www.gallup.com/cliftonstrengths/en/405590/cliftonstrengths-formerly-strengthsfinder-combinations-rare-common.aspx.

"Neurodivergence at a Glance." Imagine | Johns Hopkins University, October 5, 2022. https://imagine.jhu.edu/blog/2022/10/05/neurodivergence-at-a-glance/. Professional, Cleveland Clinic Medical. "Neurodivergent." Cleveland Clinic, March 19, 2025. https://my.clevelandclinic.org/health/symptoms/23154-neurodivergent.

"11 Neurodivergent Grammy Nominees." *ADDitude*, February 14, 2025. https://www.additudemag.com/slideshows/12-neurodivergent-grammy-nominees.

NeuroLaunch.com. "Autistic Adults Employment Rates: A Comprehensive Analysis,"
August 11, 2024. https://neurolaunch.com/
what-percentage-of-autistic-adults-are-employed.

"Research Roundup: Neurodiversity in the Workplace,
Student Financial Aid Eligibility and Guided
Pathways." Uploaded by *DC Digest* [Vilmer Alvarado].
CTE Policy Watch. Association for Career and Technical
Services, May 17, 2024.

Quinn, Jayme. "How Much of Communication Is
Nonverbal?" The University of Texas Permian
Basin (UTPB), May 15, 2023. https://online.
utpb.edu/about-us/articles/communication/
how-much-of-communication-is-nonverbal.

Rocky Mountain ADA. "Rise in Neurodiversity in the
Workplace," n.d. https://rockymountainada.org/
news/blog/rise-neurodiversity-workplace.

Sam Glenn, interview by Jocelyn Carbonara.
March 27, 2025.

Strack, Rainer, Carsten Von Der Linden, Mike Booker, and
Andrea Strohmayr. "Decoding Global Talent." *BCG
Global*, October 6, 2014. https://www.bcg.com/publi-
cations/2014/people-organization-human-
resources-decoding-global-talent.

Sutton, Robert I. *The No Asshole Rule: Building a Civilized
Workplace and Surviving One That Isn't*, 2007. https://
ci.nii.ac.jp/ncid/BB0417406X.

Wheat, Kay, Elaine Brohan, Claire Henderson, and
　　Graham Thornicroft. "Mental Illness and the
　　Workplace: Conceal or Reveal?" *Journal of the
　　Royal Society of Medicine* 103, no. 3 (March 1, 2010):
　　83–86. https://doi.org/10.1258/jrsm.2009.090317.

"Working With Claire: An Unauthorized Guide—High
　　Growth Handbook," n.d. https://growth.eladgil.com/
　　book/the-role-of-the-ceo/insights-working-with-claire.

Wyatt, Honey. "Half of Neurodivergent Employees
　　Miss Work Due to Lack of Support, Report
　　Finds." *HR Magazine*, June 2, 2024. https://
　　www.hrmagazine.co.uk/content/news/
　　half-of-neurodivergent-employees-miss-work-
　　due-to-lack-of-support-report-finds.

About the Author

With decades of experience in insurance, private practice, hospital, and medical device industries, Elisa "Lee" Judson has a panoramic view of how organizations work. Having navigated three major corporate transformations without turnover or loss in productivity from any of her high-performing teams, she has proven strengths in change management and integration. Throughout her work, she applies Six Sigma, Lean, and Kaizen principles to bolster project management and operations to cut costs and improve patient care.

But her true passion lies in helping neurodiverse teams thrive. Through her personal experience coaching neurodivergent employees and leaders—and her special relationship with the Association for Autism and Neurodiversity—Lee aims to end stigmas while equipping all team members in the process. Connect with Lee at:

www.Bridge2WorkCoaching.com

www.ingramcontent.com/pod-product-compliance
Lightning Source LLC
Chambersburg PA
CBHW031847200326
41597CB00012B/301